IMAGINE.
ACT.
INSPIRE.

A Daily Journal

Brittany Anderson
Bryan J. Sweet

ISBN-13: 978-0999504000
ISBN-10: 0-9995040-0-2

INTRODUCTION

Do you ever get to the end of your day and wonder what on earth you accomplished that day? Or do you find yourself wondering if life can get any more difficult or stressful? If so, you're not alone—we've all been there at some point in our lives. We prepared this book to provide inspiration to you each day of the year and to give you a fun, easy way to get organized and focus on the good in your life. Let's face it—if you're not having a little fun, then what's the point?!

A common mantra says that if you have too many priorities, you have none. Often, we feel defeated at the end of the day because we are trying to get too much done. Or we schedule only work-related tasks and make time for ourselves only if we can squeeze it in. By doing this, we are essentially setting ourselves up for failure.

This is where the idea for this book came along. We wanted to answer the question we've posed to ourselves many times: "How do we find something that will not only help keep you organized and set priorities but also help you get more accomplished and start each day off on a positive note?" Before we could answer that, there was one more component we wanted to answer for you.

Many of us are moving so fast that we often reflect back on the day and think, "What in the world did I even get done today?" Using this book will give you a sense of accomplishment because it will enable you to focus on the tasks that are most important.

Also, it will give you a sense of purpose and focus every day, in a very simple way. Here are the main parts of this journal.

1. Positive Quotes

Start out each day with a dose of inspiration from a positive quote. It's amazing the shift you can have in your mind-set by starting your day off with a positive thought.

Research shows that being positive produces healthy emotions. Professor Barbara Fredrickson, a social psychologist from the University of North Carolina in Chapel Hill, has researched human emotions for the past twenty-five years. She suggests that positivity is the mind-set that helps produce emotions such as joy, amusement, happiness, serenity, gratitude, and inspiration. People who prioritize positivity when they make their choices about how to arrange their day seem to benefit from more positive emotions, and they grow and become better versions of themselves over time. Dr. Fredrickson said, "If we take positive emotions more seriously and schedule our days so that we know there's certain events…if we prioritize those in our days, we do better."[1]

This journal helps you do that.

Positivity benefits our physical health, too. A 2016 study by Harvard University found that having an optimistic outlook on life—a general expectation that good things will happen—may help people live longer. The study found that women who were optimistic had a significantly reduced risk of dying from several major causes of death, including cancer, heart disease, stroke, respiratory disease, and infection—over an eight-year period, compared with women who were less optimistic. So greater optimism doesn't just make us feel

1. Lynne Malcolm, "Scientific Evidence Points to Importance of Positive Thinking," June 17, 2015, Radio National website, http://www.abc.net.au/radionational/programs/allinthemind/the-scientific-evidence-for-positive-thinking/6553614.

happier; it directly impacts our biological systems.[2] This research studied only women, but many other studies reveal similar findings for men, too.

2. Two Things You're Grateful for Each Day

Historian Alice Morse Earle said, "Every day may not be good, but there is something good in every day." End your day with the top two things you're grateful for. It could be something as simple as the sweet hug you got from your child when you got home from work. Or maybe you had the best turkey sandwich of your life for lunch. Or you got a compliment from a coworker who doesn't speak up much. When you finish your day by finding the good that happened, it helps your brain be at peace and puts you in a positive mind-set to start the next day with a smile.

Easy, right? Well, not so fast. They say it takes anywhere from twenty-one to ninety days to create a habit…so you need some accountability here. This is why we recommend that you partner with a friend, colleague, or family member and work through this daily inspiration book together. That way, you can check in with each other to make sure you've each completed your 1-2-3's for the day. Not only will it be helpful to you, but you will be helping the other person improve his or her life as well. And it can be fun to share those things you're grateful for each day. On some days, you might find that you are just thankful you have an accountability partner to keep you focused!

3. Your Top Three "To-Do" Items for Each Day

Yes, you're limited to three. Why, you ask? Remember, we mentioned earlier that if you have

---

2. "Karen Feldscher, "How Power of Positive Thinking Works," December 7, 2016, *HarvardGazette*, Harvard University website, http://news.harvard.edu/gazette/story/2016/12/optistic-women-live-longer-are-healthier/.

too many priorities, you have none. This will help you focus on your top priorities and keep you from feeling overwhelmed. These should be the three tasks that are so important that if you didn't get them done, it would keep you up at night.

The old saying goes, "Monkey see, monkey do." We typically heard that as children, when we were being taught the importance of setting a good example for others. As adults, there is a different saying involving monkeys. Studies have shown if you end your day by jotting down your top priorities for the following day, the "monkeys" will go to work in your brain and subconsciously start coming up with solutions for getting your top tasks accomplished.

If you go to bed leaving your slate for tomorrow open-ended and unplanned, the monkeys do some damage by creating a bunch of noise and keeping you up at night because you don't have key tasks to focus on. This book helps you get those monkeys in motion.

Here's a little "insider" tip. You know those top to-do's we told you to identify for the following day? To be most effective and efficient, *start* your day by accomplishing the top items you deemed most important…before you do anything else, focus on the things you've deemed most important, and you will start your day on a positive note!

Think about it this way. Simply by completing three top priorities each day, you are accomplishing 1,095 important tasks in a year. Imagine the positive results this will have on your life in just one year!

4. Random Acts of Kindness

We have placed, randomly throughout this book,

suggestions for random acts of kindness you can do for others. Doing kind things for others, often unexpectedly, is one of life's greatest pleasures. Recent research shows that when we do good for others, we benefit from a "helper's high."

Doing good has been shown to decrease stress, increase life expectancy, make us feel better and happier at work, promote mental health, and motivate us to do good again.[3]

This book also contains "Notes" pages for journaling. The biggest lie we tell ourselves is, "I'll remember that." But our minds are so full of details, sometimes we forget things. It's good to get into the habit of jotting thoughts down as they come to you because writing down your hopes and dreams will help manifest them. Then take it one step further and review your journal entries often! Zig Ziglar said it best: "People often say that motivation doesn't last. Well, neither does bathing. That's why we recommend it daily."

We hope you enjoy your journey through the next 365 days.

Imagine the impact you can have on yourself and others by living a life of gratitude and consciously "paying it forward."

Act on your three most important to-do's every day.

Inspire yourself and others by living a life of purpose. Read and share uplifting quotes from people who have made notable contributions to society, and write down the things you are most grateful for every day.

Let's get started!

3. "7 Scientific Facts about the Benefit of Doing Good," Goodnet.org, January 26, 2017, http://www.goodnet.org/articles/7-scientific-facts-about-benefit-doing-good.

WHEN I GET **SAD**, I **STOP** BEING SAD AND **BE AWESOME** INSTEAD.

~Barney Stinson
Character on *How I Met Your Mother*

TWO AREAS OF **GRATITUDE**

TOP THREE **TO-DO'S** FOR TODAY

1. _____
2. _____
3. _____

THE ONLY WAY TO DO **GREAT WORK** IS TO **LOVE WHAT YOU DO**. IF YOU HAVEN'T FOUND IT YET, **KEEP LOOKING**. DON'T SETTLE. AS WITH ALL MATTERS OF THE HEART, YOU'LL **KNOW** WHEN YOU **FIND IT**.

~Steve Jobs
Cofounder, Chairman, and CEO, Apple Inc.

TWO AREAS OF **GRATITUDE**

TOP THREE **TO-DO'S** FOR TODAY

1. _____
2. _____
3. _____

EVERY DAY
MAY **NOT** BE **GOOD**,
BUT THERE IS
SOMETHING GOOD
IN **EVERY** DAY.

~Unknown

TWO AREAS OF **GRATITUDE**

TOP THREE **TO-DO'S** FOR TODAY

1. _____

2. _____

3. _____

WHOEVER IS **HAPPY** WILL MAKE OTHERS **HAPPY,** TOO.

~Mark Twain
Writer

TWO AREAS OF **GRATITUDE**

TOP THREE **TO-DO'S** FOR TODAY

1. _____

2. _____

3. _____

ANYTHING
WORTH DOING
IS WORTH
OVERDOING.

~Mick Jagger
Lead Singer, The Rolling Stones

TWO AREAS OF **GRATITUDE**

TOP THREE **TO-DO'S** FOR TODAY

1. _____

2. _____

3. _____

DAY 6: DATE: _____

THOSE WHO BRING
SUNSHINE
INTO THE **LIVES** OF **OTHERS**
CANNOT **KEEP IT** FOR
THEMSELVES.

~J. M. Barrie
Scottish Writer and Creator of *Peter Pan*

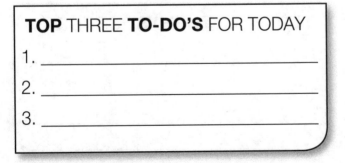

TWO AREAS OF **GRATITUDE**

TOP THREE **TO-DO'S** FOR TODAY

1. _____

2. _____

3. _____

PEOPLE SAY THAT **MONEY** IS **NOT** THE **KEY** TO **HAPPINESS,** BUT I ALWAYS FIGURED IF YOU HAVE ENOUGH **MONEY,** YOU CAN HAVE A **KEY** MADE.

~Joan Rivers
Comedienne

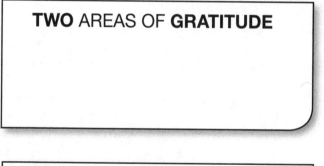

TWO AREAS OF **GRATITUDE**

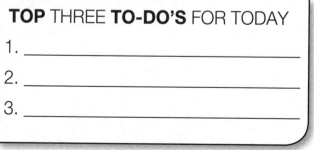

TOP THREE **TO-DO'S** FOR TODAY

1. _____
2. _____
3. _____

RANDOM **ACT** OF **KINDNESS**

COMPLIMENT YOUR
SIGNIFICANT OTHER
OR SOMEONE **CLOSE** TO YOU.

EVERYBODY
IS A **GENIUS**.
BUT IF YOU JUDGE A **FISH** BY ITS **ABILITY TO CLIMB A TREE,** IT WILL LIVE ITS **WHOLE LIFE** BELIEVING THAT IT IS **STUPID**.

~Albert Einstein
Theoretical Physicist

TWO AREAS OF **GRATITUDE**

TOP THREE **TO-DO'S** FOR TODAY

1. _____
2. _____
3. _____

YOU ARE *MORE* THAN
GOOD ENOUGH.

~Unknown

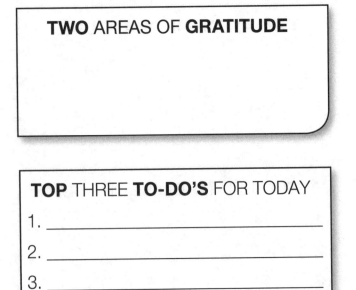

TWO AREAS OF **GRATITUDE**

TOP THREE **TO-DO'S** FOR TODAY

1. _____

2. _____

3. _____

WE DON'T **KNOW** WHO **WE ARE** UNTIL WE **SEE** WHAT WE CAN **DO**.

~Martha Grimes
Writer of Detective Fiction

TWO AREAS OF **GRATITUDE**

TOP THREE **TO-DO'S** FOR TODAY

1. _____

2. _____

3. _____

REMEMBER THAT SOMETIMES **NOT** GETTING WHAT YOU **WANT** IS A **WONDERFUL** STROKE OF **LUCK**.

~Lhamo Dondrub
The 14th Dalai Lama

TWO AREAS OF **GRATITUDE**

TOP THREE **TO-DO'S** FOR TODAY

1. _____
2. _____
3. _____

PASSION IS ENERGY.
FEEL THE POWER
THAT COMES FROM
FOCUSING ON
WHAT EXCITES YOU.

~Oprah Winfrey
Media Proprietor

TWO AREAS OF **GRATITUDE**

TOP THREE **TO-DO'S** FOR TODAY

1. _____

2. _____

3. _____

LIFE ISN'T ABOUT FINDING YOURSELF. LIFE IS ABOUT CREATING YOURSELF.

~George Bernard Shaw
Irish Playwright

TWO AREAS OF **GRATITUDE**

TOP THREE **TO-DO'S** FOR TODAY

1. _____

2. _____

3. _____

WHENEVER POSSIBLE, **STOP** AND **TRULY LISTEN** TO THOSE AROUND YOU. IT COULD BE A **COWORKER** OR A **CLOSE FRIEND**, BUT THE POINT IS TO **CONNECT** AND **HEAR** WHAT'S ON **THEIR MINDS**, INSTEAD OF JUST WAITING FOR **YOUR TURN** TO TALK.

~Unknown

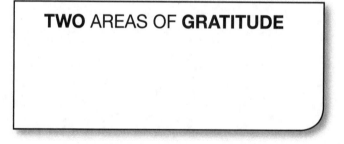

TWO AREAS OF **GRATITUDE**

TOP THREE **TO-DO'S** FOR TODAY

1. _____

2. _____

3. _____

NOTES

WORRY IS THE INTEREST PAID BY THOSE WHO **BORROW TROUBLE**.

~George Washington
First US President

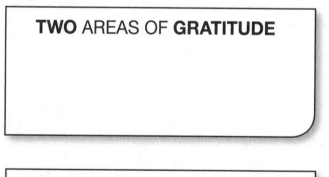

TWO AREAS OF **GRATITUDE**

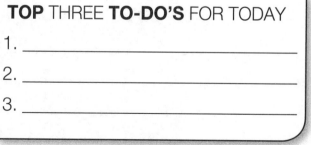

TOP THREE **TO-DO'S** FOR TODAY

1. _____

2. _____

3. _____

HAPPINESS IS **NOT** A DESTINATION. IT IS A **METHOD** OF LIFE.

~Burton Hills
Quote Writer

TWO AREAS OF **GRATITUDE**

TOP THREE **TO-DO'S** FOR TODAY

1. _____

2. _____

3. _____

THE **GREATEST** DISCOVERY OF MY GENERATION IS THAT A HUMAN BEING CAN **ALTER HIS LIFE** BY ALTERING HIS **ATTITUDES** OF **MIND**.

~William James
American Psychologist and Physician

TWO AREAS OF **GRATITUDE**

TOP THREE **TO-DO'S** FOR TODAY

1. _____

2. _____

3. _____

THE **GOAL** OF THIS **HUMAN** ADVENTURE IS PRODUCTIVITY — PURSUING THE FULL **DEVELOPMENT** OF ALL YOUR **POTENTIAL**.

~Jim Rohn
Motivational Speaker and Author

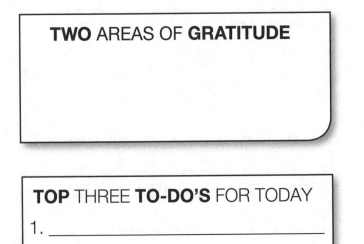

TWO AREAS OF **GRATITUDE**

TOP THREE **TO-DO'S** FOR TODAY

1. _____
2. _____
3. _____

IF WE'D ONLY **STOP** TRYING TO BE **HAPPY**, WE'D HAVE A PRETTY **GOOD** TIME.

~Edith Wharton
Novelist and Short-Story Writer

TWO AREAS OF **GRATITUDE**

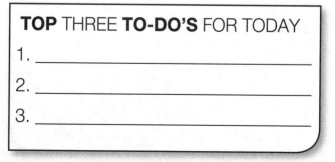

TOP THREE **TO-DO'S** FOR TODAY

1. _____
2. _____
3. _____

HAPPINESS
OFTEN SNEAKS IN THROUGH A **DOOR** YOU DIDN'T KNOW YOU **LEFT OPEN**.

~John Barrymore
Actor

TWO AREAS OF **GRATITUDE**

TOP THREE **TO-DO'S** FOR TODAY

1. _____

2. _____

3. _____

IF I HAD TO **LIVE** MY LIFE **AGAIN**, I'D MAKE THE SAME **MISTAKES**, ONLY **SOONER**.

~Tallulah Bankhead
Actress

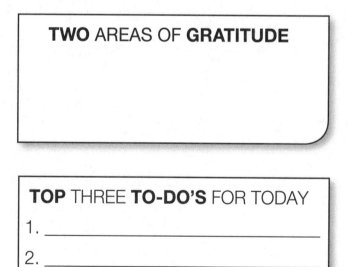

TWO AREAS OF **GRATITUDE**

TOP THREE **TO-DO'S** FOR TODAY

1. _____
2. _____
3. _____

RANDOM **ACT** OF **KINDNESS**

LEAVE LETTERS OF **ENCOURAGEMENT** ON PEOPLE'S **CARS**.

IT **DOESN'T** MATTER WHERE YOU'VE **BEEN**; IT **ONLY** MATTERS WHERE **YOU ARE GOING.**

~Brian Tracy
Motivational Speaker

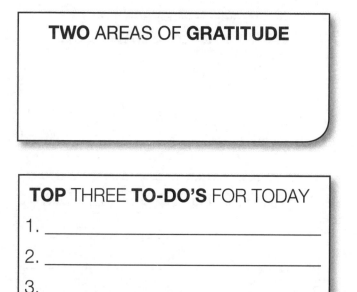

TWO AREAS OF **GRATITUDE**

TOP THREE **TO-DO'S** FOR TODAY

1. _____

2. _____

3. _____

IT'S **NOT** WHAT HAPPENS **TO** YOU, BUT HOW YOU **REACT** TO IT THAT MATTERS.

~Epictetus
Stoic Philosopher

TWO AREAS OF **GRATITUDE**

TOP THREE **TO-DO'S** FOR TODAY

1. _____
2. _____
3. _____

I'VE **NEVER** BEEN A **MILLIONAIRE,** BUT I KNOW I'D BE JUST **DARLING** AT IT.

~Dorothy Parker
Writer and Satirist

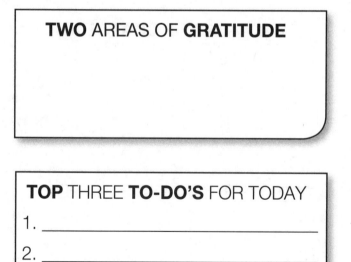

TWO AREAS OF **GRATITUDE**

TOP THREE **TO-DO'S** FOR TODAY

1. _____
2. _____
3. _____

THE **BIG SECRET** IN LIFE IS THAT THERE IS **NO** BIG SECRET. WHATEVER YOUR **GOAL**, YOU CAN GET THERE IF YOU'RE **WILLING TO WORK**.

~Opray Winfrey
Media Proprietor

TWO AREAS OF **GRATITUDE**

TOP THREE **TO-DO'S** FOR TODAY

1. _____

2. _____

3. _____

APPRECIATION
IS A **WONDERFUL** THING. IT MAKES WHAT IS **EXCELLENT** IN OTHERS BELONG **TO US** AS WELL.

Voltaire
French Enlightenment Writer and Philosopher

TWO AREAS OF **GRATITUDE**

TOP THREE **TO-DO'S** FOR TODAY

1. _____
2. _____
3. _____

DAY 27: DATE: _____

IT'S YOUR **OUTLOOK ON LIFE** THAT COUNTS. IF YOU TAKE YOURSELF **LIGHTLY** AND **DON'T** TAKE YOURSELF TOO **SERIOUSLY,** PRETTY SOON YOU CAN FIND THE **HUMOR** IN OUR **EVERYDAY** LIVES. AND SOMETIMES IT CAN BE A **LIFESAVER**.

Betty White
Actress with the Longest TV Career
of a Female Entertainer

TWO AREAS OF **GRATITUDE**

TOP THREE **TO-DO'S** FOR TODAY

1. _____

2. _____

3. _____

NEVER **DOWNPLAY** THE **TALENTS** AND **SKILLS** YOU HAVE. NO MATTER HOW **LARGE** OR SMALL THEY ARE, YOU HAVE **THE RIGHT TO BE PROUD!**

Unknown

TWO AREAS OF **GRATITUDE**

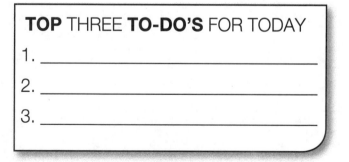

TOP THREE **TO-DO'S** FOR TODAY

1. _____

2. _____

3. _____

NOTES

DAY 29: DATE: _____

TAKE **CHANCES**, **MAKE** MISTAKES. THAT'S HOW YOU **GROW**.

Mary Tyler Moore
Sitcom Actress

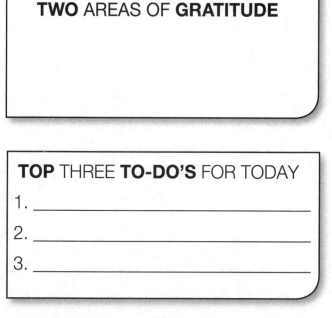

TWO AREAS OF **GRATITUDE**

TOP THREE **TO-DO'S** FOR TODAY

1. _____

2. _____

3. _____

WHEN I STARTED **COUNTING** MY BLESSINGS, MY WHOLE **LIFE** TURNED AROUND.

Willie Nelson
Musician, Singer, and Songwriter

TWO AREAS OF **GRATITUDE**

TOP THREE **TO-DO'S** FOR TODAY

1. _____

2. _____

3. _____

BUILDING A BETTER **YOU** IS THE **FIRST STEP** TO BUILDING A BETTER **AMERICA**.

Zig Ziglar
Motivational Speaker

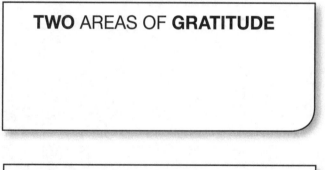

TWO AREAS OF **GRATITUDE**

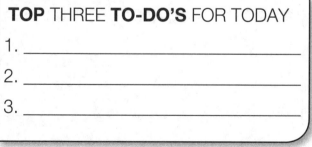

TOP THREE **TO-DO'S** FOR TODAY

1. _____

2. _____

3. _____

THE FUTURE
BELONGS TO THOSE WHO **BELIEVE** IN THE **BEAUTY** OF THEIR **DREAMS**.

Eleanor Roosevelt
Longest-Serving First Lady of the United States

TWO AREAS OF **GRATITUDE**

TOP THREE **TO-DO'S** FOR TODAY

1. _____
2. _____
3. _____

JOY IS NOT IN **THINGS**;
IT IS IN **US**.

Richard Wagner
German Opera Composer and Conductor

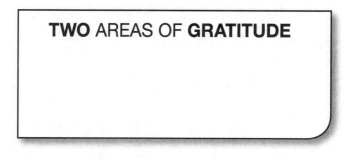

TWO AREAS OF **GRATITUDE**

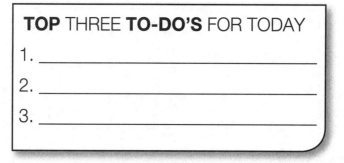

TOP THREE **TO-DO'S** FOR TODAY

1. _____

2. _____

3. _____

WHEN IT COMES TO **LIFE**, THE **CRITICAL** THING IS WHETHER YOU **TAKE** THINGS FOR **GRANTED** OR **TAKE** THEM WITH GRATITUDE.

G. K. Chesterton
English Writer

TWO AREAS OF **GRATITUDE**

TOP THREE **TO-DO'S** FOR TODAY

1. _____
2. _____
3. _____

TO LIVE ON **PURPOSE,** FOLLOW YOUR **HEART** AND **LIVE** YOUR **DREAMS**.

Marcia Wieder
Professional Speaker and Author

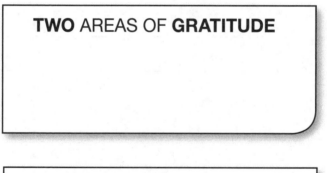

TWO AREAS OF **GRATITUDE**

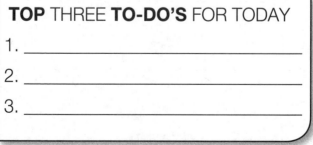

TOP THREE **TO-DO'S** FOR TODAY

1. _____
2. _____
3. _____

RANDOM **ACT** OF **KINDNESS**

PAY FOR SOMEONE'S **MEAL** AT A RESTAURANT.

LIFE IS SHORT —
AVOID CAUSING YAWNS.

Elinor Glyn
British Novelist and Scriptwriter

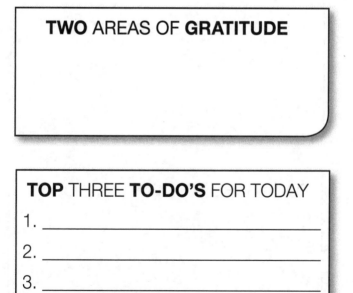

TWO AREAS OF **GRATITUDE**

TOP THREE **TO-DO'S** FOR TODAY

1. _____

2. _____

3. _____

IF YOU **OBEY** ALL THE RULES, YOU **MISS** ALL THE **FUN**.

Katharine Hepburn
Actress

TWO AREAS OF **GRATITUDE**

TOP THREE **TO-DO'S** FOR TODAY

1. _____
2. _____
3. _____

IT **ALWAYS** SEEMS **IMPOSSIBLE** UNTIL IT IS **DONE**.

Nelson Mandela
South African Anti-Apartheid Revolutionary

TWO AREAS OF **GRATITUDE**

TOP THREE **TO-DO'S** FOR TODAY

1. _____
2. _____
3. _____

TRUST **UNCERTAINTY** TO BRING YOU TO **CLARITY.**

Joanna Swanger
Professor at Earlham College

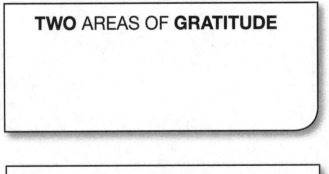

TWO AREAS OF **GRATITUDE**

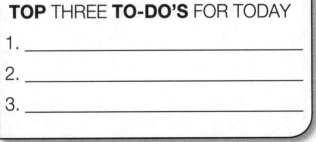

TOP THREE **TO-DO'S** FOR TODAY

1. _____
2. _____
3. _____

WHEREVER YOU GO, GO WITH **ALL** YOUR **HEART**.

Confucius
Chinese Philosopher

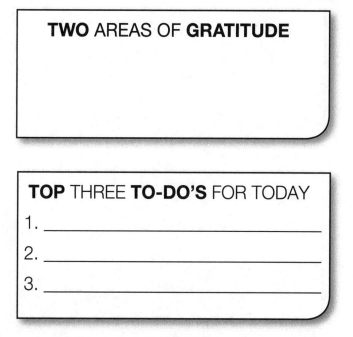

TWO AREAS OF **GRATITUDE**

TOP THREE **TO-DO'S** FOR TODAY

1. _____
2. _____
3. _____

BE BOLD.
IF YOU'RE GOING TO MAKE AN **ERROR**,
MAKE A DOOZEY,
AND **DON'T** BE **AFRAID**
TO **HIT** THE BALL.

Billie Jean King
Former World No. 1 Professional Tennis Player

TWO AREAS OF **GRATITUDE**

TOP THREE **TO-DO'S** FOR TODAY

1. _____

2. _____

3. _____

WHEN YOU GET TO THE **END** OF YOUR **ROPE**, TIE A **KNOT** IN IT AND **HANG** ON.

Franklin D. Roosevelt
32nd US President

TWO AREAS OF **GRATITUDE**

TOP THREE **TO-DO'S** FOR TODAY

1. _____
2. _____
3. _____

NOTES

DAY 43: DATE: _____

WHATEVER YOU ARE, BE A **GOOD** ONE.

Abraham Lincoln
16th US President

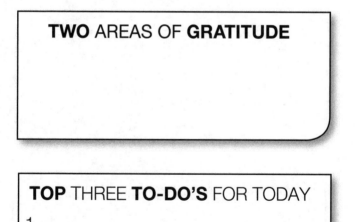

TWO AREAS OF **GRATITUDE**

TOP THREE **TO-DO'S** FOR TODAY

1. _____
2. _____
3. _____

THOSE WHO **DON'T** BELIEVE IN **MAGIC** WILL **NEVER FIND** IT.

Roald Dahl
British Writer and Fighter Pilot

TWO AREAS OF **GRATITUDE**

TOP THREE **TO-DO'S** FOR TODAY

1. _____

2. _____

3. _____

THERE ARE **TWO** KINDS OF PEOPLE: **THOSE WHO DO** THE **WORK** AND THOSE WHO **TAKE THE CREDIT**. TRY TO BE IN THE **FIRST** GROUP; THERE IS LESS **COMPETITION** THERE.

Indira Gandhi
The Only Female to Serve as
Prime Minister of India

TWO AREAS OF **GRATITUDE**

TOP THREE **TO-DO'S** FOR TODAY

1. _____

2. _____

3. _____

KEEP YOUR **FACE** TO THE **SUNSHINE**, AND YOU **CANNOT** SEE THE **SHADOW**.

Helen Keller
Writer and Political Activist

TWO AREAS OF **GRATITUDE**

TOP THREE **TO-DO'S** FOR TODAY

1. _____

2. _____

3. _____

IF YOU HAVE AN **IDEA**, THAT'S GOOD.
IF YOU **ALSO** HAVE AN **IDEA** AS TO **HOW** TO **WORK** IT OUT, THAT'S BETTER.

Henry Ford
Industrialist and Founder of the
Ford Motor Company

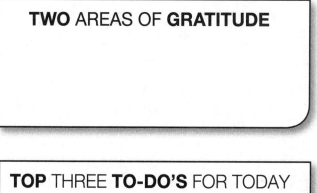

TWO AREAS OF **GRATITUDE**

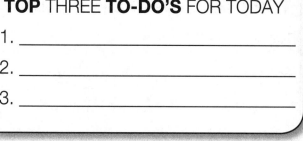

TOP THREE **TO-DO'S** FOR TODAY

1. _____

2. _____

3. _____

THE ONE **IMPORTANT** THING I HAVE **LEARNED** OVER THE YEARS IS THE DIFFERENCE BETWEEN TAKING ONE'S **WORK** SERIOUSLY AND TAKING ONE'S **SELF** SERIOUSLY. THE FIRST IS **IMPERATIVE**, AND THE SECOND IS **DISASTROUS**.

Margot Fonteyn
English Ballerina with the Royal Ballet

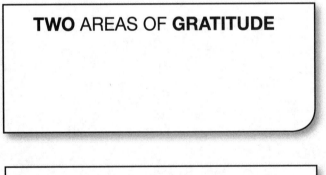

TWO AREAS OF **GRATITUDE**

TOP THREE **TO-DO'S** FOR TODAY

1. _____

2. _____

3. _____

DAY 49: DATE: _____

YOUR LIFE IS **NOT** A **PROBLEM** TO BE **SOLVED** BUT A **GIFT** TO BE **OPENED**.

Wayne Muller
Speaker, Author, and Minister

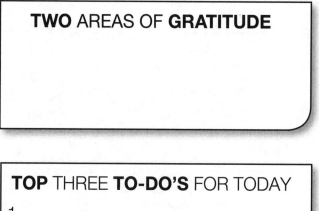

TWO AREAS OF **GRATITUDE**

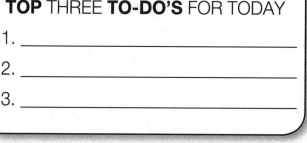

TOP THREE **TO-DO'S** FOR TODAY

1. _____
2. _____
3. _____

RANDOM **ACT** OF **KINDNESS**

WRITE A HAND-WRITTEN LETTER TO A **FORMER TEACHER** WHO HAD A BIG IMPACT IN YOUR LIFE.

WHEN THE **STUDENT** IS **READY**, THE **TEACHER** APPEARS.

Buddhist Saying

TWO AREAS OF **GRATITUDE**

TOP THREE **TO-DO'S** FOR TODAY

1. _____
2. _____
3. _____

NOTHING **GREAT** WAS EVER **ACHIEVED** WITHOUT **ENTHUSIASM**.

Ralph Waldo Emerson
Essayist, Lecturer, and Poet

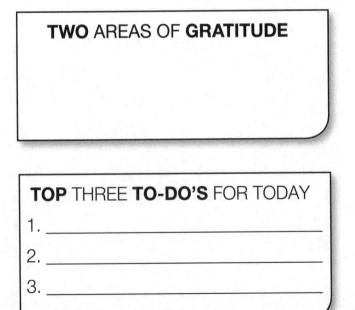

TWO AREAS OF **GRATITUDE**

TOP THREE **TO-DO'S** FOR TODAY

1. _____

2. _____

3. _____

A LIFETIME
CAN WELL BE SPENT
CORRECTING AND **IMPROVING**
ONE'S OWN **FAULTS**
WITHOUT **BOTHERING**
ABOUT OTHERS.

Edward Weston
20th-Century Photographer

TWO AREAS OF **GRATITUDE**

TOP THREE **TO-DO'S** FOR TODAY

1. _____

2. _____

3. _____

KINDNESS IN **WORDS** CREATES **CONFIDENCE**. KINDNESS IN **THINKING** CREATES **PROFOUNDNESS**. KINDNESS IN GIVING CREATES **LOVE**.

Lao Tzu
Ancient Chinese Philosopher

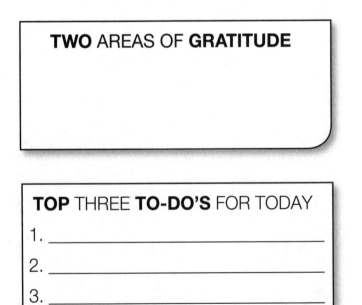

TWO AREAS OF **GRATITUDE**

TOP THREE **TO-DO'S** FOR TODAY

1. _____

2. _____

3. _____

PEOPLE DO **BEST**
WHAT COMES **NATURALLY**.

John F. Kennedy
35th US President

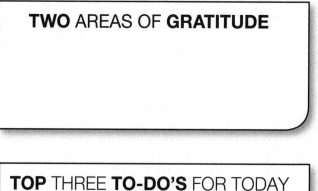

TWO AREAS OF **GRATITUDE**

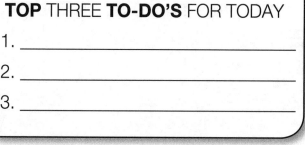

TOP THREE **TO-DO'S** FOR TODAY

1. _____
2. _____
3. _____

HAPPINESS
IS ESSENTIALLY A **STATE** OF **GOING** SOMEWHERE **WHOLEHEARTEDLY**, ONE-DIRECTIONALLY, WITHOUT **REGRET** OR **RESERVATION**.

W. H. Sheldon
Psychologist

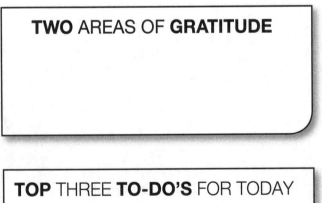

TWO AREAS OF **GRATITUDE**

TOP THREE **TO-DO'S** FOR TODAY

1. _____

2. _____

3. _____

AH, BUT A MAN'S **REACH** SHOULD **EXCEED** HIS **GRASP**, OR WHAT'S A **HEAVEN** FOR?

Robert Browning
English Poet and Playwright

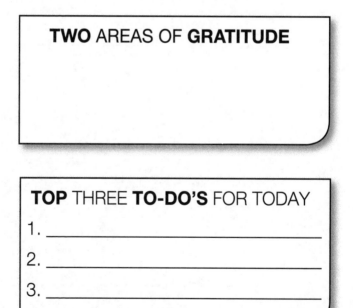

TWO AREAS OF **GRATITUDE**

TOP THREE **TO-DO'S** FOR TODAY

1. _____

2. _____

3. _____

NOTES

OUR GREATEST WEARINESS COMES FROM **WORK** NOT DONE.

Eric Hoffer
Moral and Social Philosopher

TWO AREAS OF **GRATITUDE**

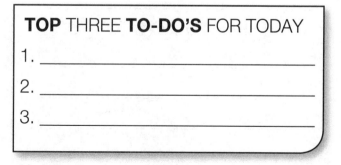

TOP THREE **TO-DO'S** FOR TODAY

1. _____

2. _____

3. _____

WE ARE WHAT WE REPEATEDLY DO. EXCELLENCE, THEN, IS NOT AN **ACT**, BUT A **HABIT**.

Aristotle
Ancient Greek Philosopher and Scientist

TWO AREAS OF **GRATITUDE**

TOP THREE **TO-DO'S** FOR TODAY

1. _____
2. _____
3. _____

HOLDING ON TO **ANGER** IS LIKE GRASPING A **HOT COAL** WITH THE INTENT OF **THROWING** IT AT SOMEONE ELSE; **YOU** ARE THE ONE WHO GETS **BURNED**.

Buddha
Nepalese Ascetic and Sage

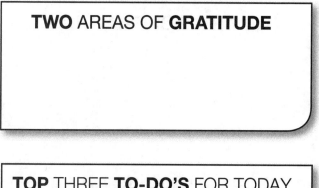

TWO AREAS OF **GRATITUDE**

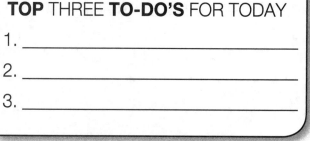

TOP THREE **TO-DO'S** FOR TODAY

1. _____
2. _____
3. _____

WE DON'T **LAUGH** BECAUSE WE'RE **HAPPY**; WE'RE **HAPPY** BECAUSE WE **LAUGH**.

William James
Philosopher, Psychologist, and Physician

TWO AREAS OF **GRATITUDE**

TOP THREE **TO-DO'S** FOR TODAY

1. _____
2. _____
3. _____

DAY 61: DATE: _____

I HAVE FOUND THAT **MOST** PEOPLE ARE ABOUT AS **HAPPY** AS THEY **MAKE** UP THEIR **MINDS** TO BE.

Abraham Lincoln
16th US President

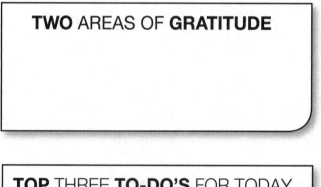

TWO AREAS OF **GRATITUDE**

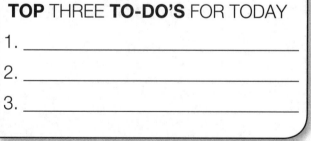

TOP THREE **TO-DO'S** FOR TODAY

1. _____
2. _____
3. _____

THE **GREAT** THING IN THIS WORLD IS **NOT** SO MUCH **WHERE** WE STAND AS IN WHAT **DIRECTION** WE ARE **MOVING**.

Oliver Wendell Holmes, Sr.
Physician, Poet, and Polymath

TWO AREAS OF **GRATITUDE**

TOP THREE **TO-DO'S** FOR TODAY

1. _____
2. _____
3. _____

IF YOU MAKE IT A **HABIT** **NOT** TO BLAME OTHERS, YOU WILL FEEL THE **GROWTH** OF THE **ABILITY** TO **LOVE** IN YOUR SOUL, AND YOU WILL SEE THE **GROWTH** OF **GOODNESS** IN YOUR LIFE.

Leo Tolstoy
Russian Writer

TWO AREAS OF **GRATITUDE**

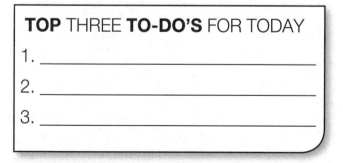

TOP THREE **TO-DO'S** FOR TODAY

1. _____
2. _____
3. _____

RANDOM **ACT** OF **KINDNESS**

DO A **FAVOR** WITHOUT ASKING FOR ANYTHING IN RETURN.

ASSOCIATE WITH PEOPLE WHO ARE **LIKELY** TO **IMPROVE** YOU.

Seneca
Roman Stoic Philosopher

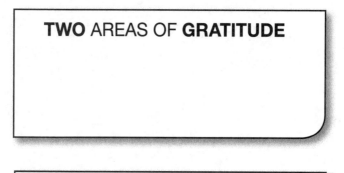

TWO AREAS OF **GRATITUDE**

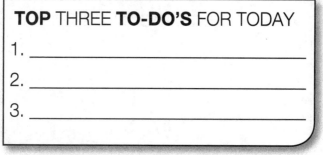

TOP THREE **TO-DO'S** FOR TODAY

1. _____
2. _____
3. _____

DO NOT **SPOIL** WHAT YOU **HAVE** BY **DESIRING** WHAT YOU HAVE **NOT**, BUT REMEMBER THAT WHAT YOU **NOW** HAVE WAS ONCE AMONG THE THINGS ONLY **HOPED** FOR.

Epicurus
Ancient Greek Philosopher

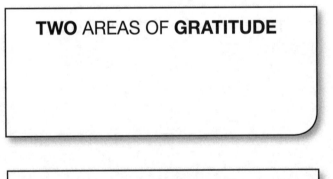

TWO AREAS OF **GRATITUDE**

TOP THREE **TO-DO'S** FOR TODAY

1. _____

2. _____

3. _____

NOTHING CAN MAKE OUR **LIFE**, OR THE **LIVES** OF OTHER PEOPLE, MORE **BEAUTIFUL** THAN PERPETUAL **KINDNESS**.

Leo Tolstoy
Russian Writer

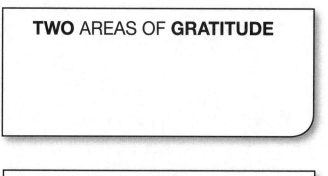

TWO AREAS OF **GRATITUDE**

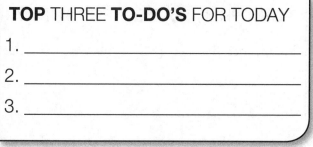

TOP THREE **TO-DO'S** FOR TODAY

1. _____

2. _____

3. _____

OPTIMISM IS TRUE MORAL **COURAGE.**

Ernest Shakleton
British Explorer of the Antarctic

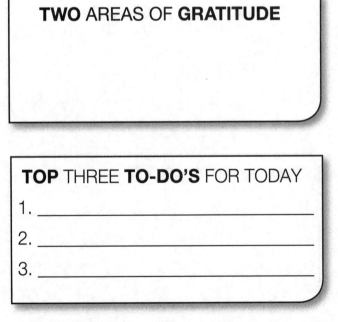

TWO AREAS OF **GRATITUDE**

TOP THREE **TO-DO'S** FOR TODAY

1. _____
2. _____
3. _____

WHATEVER IS **WORTH** DOING AT ALL IS **WORTH** DOING **WELL**.

Lord Chesterfield
British Statesman

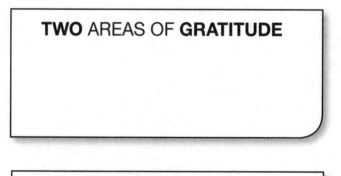

TWO AREAS OF **GRATITUDE**

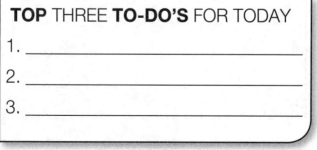

TOP THREE **TO-DO'S** FOR TODAY

1. _____
2. _____
3. _____

ONE OF THE **BEST** AND FASTEST WAYS OF **ACQUIRING** KNOWLEDGE IS TO **INSIST** ON REMAINING I G N O R A N T ABOUT THINGS THAT **AREN'T WORTH KNOWING.**

Sydney Harris
Journalist

TWO AREAS OF **GRATITUDE**

TOP THREE **TO-DO'S** FOR TODAY

1. _____

2. _____

3. _____

THE **BEST** WAY TO CHEER YOURSELF IS TO TRY TO **CHEER** SOMEBODY ELSE UP.

Mark Twain
Writer

TWO AREAS OF **GRATITUDE**

TOP THREE **TO-DO'S** FOR TODAY

1. _____

2. _____

3. _____

NOTES

WHEN YOU ARE **CONTENT** TO BE SIMPLY YOURSELF AND DON'T **COMPARE** OR **COMPETE**, EVERYBODY WILL **RESPECT** YOU.

Lao Tzu
Ancient Chinese Philosopher

TWO AREAS OF **GRATITUDE**

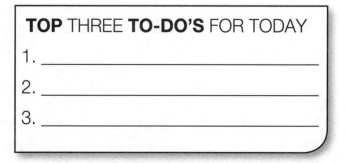

TOP THREE **TO-DO'S** FOR TODAY

1. _____
2. _____
3. _____

IRON **RUSTS** FROM **DISUSE**, **STAGNANT** WATER LOSES ITS **PURITY**, AND IN **COLD** WEATHER BECOMES **FROZEN**; EVEN SO DOES **INACTION** SAP THE VIGOR OF THE **MIND**.

Leonardo da Vinci
Italian Artist

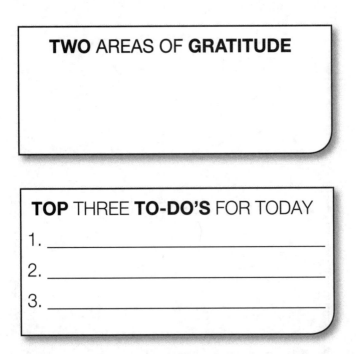

TWO AREAS OF **GRATITUDE**

TOP THREE **TO-DO'S** FOR TODAY

1. _____

2. _____

3. _____

BETTER TO **CHASE** A DREAM THAN TO BE **PURSUED** BY **REGRETS.**

Harvey Mackay
Businessman and Author

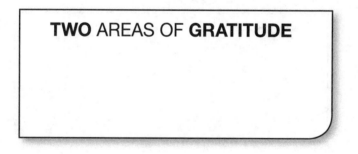

TWO AREAS OF **GRATITUDE**

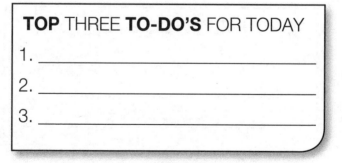

TOP THREE **TO-DO'S** FOR TODAY

1. _____

2. _____

3. _____

BE A PINEAPPLE: STAND **TALL,** WEAR A **CROWN,** AND BE **SWEET** ON THE **INSIDE**.

Unknown

TWO AREAS OF **GRATITUDE**

TOP THREE **TO-DO'S** FOR TODAY

1. _____

2. _____

3. _____

NO MATTER HOW YOU **FEEL**, GET UP, DRESS UP, SHOW UP, **AND** NEVER **GIVE** UP.

Unknown

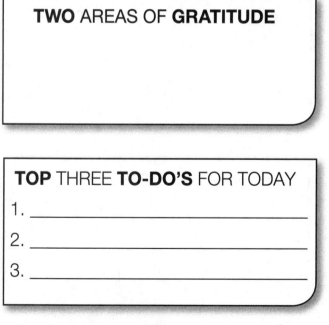

TWO AREAS OF **GRATITUDE**

TOP THREE **TO-DO'S** FOR TODAY

1. _____

2. _____

3. _____

BELIEVE YOU **CAN**,
AND YOU'RE HALFWAY THERE.

Theodore Roosevelt
26th US President

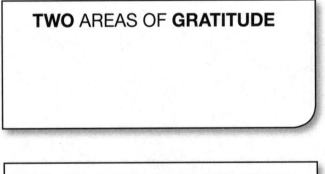

TWO AREAS OF **GRATITUDE**

TOP THREE **TO-DO'S** FOR TODAY

1. _____

2. _____

3. _____

THE **SECRET** OF HAVING IT ALL IS TO **BELIEVE** YOU **ALREADY** DO.

Unknown

TWO AREAS OF **GRATITUDE**

TOP THREE **TO-DO'S** FOR TODAY

1. _____

2. _____

3. _____

RANDOM **ACT** OF **KINDNESS**

SPEND **TIME** WITH YOUR **GRANDPARENTS.**

YOU DON'T INSPIRE OTHERS BY BEING **PERFECT**. YOU **INSPIRE** THEM BY HOW YOU **DEAL** WITH IMPERFECTIONS.

Unknown

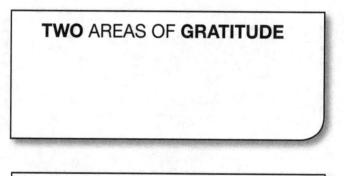

TWO AREAS OF **GRATITUDE**

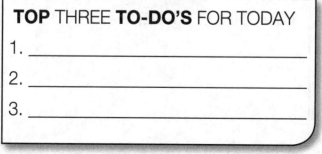

TOP THREE **TO-DO'S** FOR TODAY

1. _____

2. _____

3. _____

THE PEOPLE WHO ARE **CRAZY** ENOUGH TO **THINK** THEY CAN **CHANGE** THE **WORLD** ARE THE ONES WHO **DO**.

Steve Jobs
Cofounder, Chairman, and CEO, Apple Inc.

TWO AREAS OF **GRATITUDE**

TOP THREE **TO-DO'S** FOR TODAY

1. _____
2. _____
3. _____

IF YOU ARE **NOT** OBSESSED WITH THE **LIFE** YOU ARE **LIVING**, CHANGE IT.

Unknown

TWO AREAS OF **GRATITUDE**

TOP THREE **TO-DO'S** FOR TODAY

1. _____

2. _____

3. _____

SUCCESS ISN'T JUST ABOUT WHAT YOU ACCOMPLISH IN **YOUR** LIFE. IT'S ABOUT WHAT YOU INSPIRE **OTHERS** TO DO.

Unknown

TWO AREAS OF **GRATITUDE**

TOP THREE **TO-DO'S** FOR TODAY

1. _____

2. _____

3. _____

LIFE'S MOST **PERSISTENT** AND **URGENT** QUESTION IS, 'WHAT ARE YOU DOING FOR OTHERS?'

Martin Luther King, Jr.
Baptist Minister and Civil Rights Activist

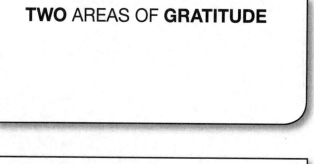

TWO AREAS OF **GRATITUDE**

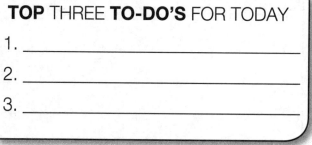

TOP THREE **TO-DO'S** FOR TODAY

1. _____

2. _____

3. _____

DO WHAT YOU HAVE TO DO UNTIL YOU CAN **DO** WHAT YOU **WANT** TO DO.

Oprah Winfrey
Media Proprietor

TWO AREAS OF **GRATITUDE**

TOP THREE **TO-DO'S** FOR TODAY

1. _____
2. _____
3. _____

IF YOU CAN'T FIGURE OUT YOUR PURPOSE, FIGURE OUT YOUR **PASSION**. YOUR PASSION WILL **LEAD** YOU DIRECTLY TO YOUR **PURPOSE**.

T. D. Jakes
Megachurch Pastor, Author, and Filmmaker

TWO AREAS OF **GRATITUDE**

TOP THREE **TO-DO'S** FOR TODAY

1. _____

2. _____

3. _____

NOTES

YOU WERE **BORN** WITH THE ABILITY TO **CHANGE** SOMEONE'S LIFE. DON'T EVER **WASTE** IT.

Dale Partridge
Business Coach, Speaker, and Writer

TWO AREAS OF **GRATITUDE**

TOP THREE **TO-DO'S** FOR TODAY

1. _____
2. _____
3. _____

TRADE YOUR **EXPECTATION** FOR **APPRECIATION**, AND THE WORLD CHANGES **INSTANTLY**.

Tony Robbins
Motivational Speaker and Change Catalyst

TWO AREAS OF **GRATITUDE**

TOP THREE **TO-DO'S** FOR TODAY

1. _____

2. _____

3. _____

THE KEY TO HAPPINESS IS LETTING EACH SITUATION BE **WHAT IT IS** INSTEAD OF WHAT YOU **THINK** IT SHOULD BE.

Mandy Hale
Author and The Single Woman

TWO AREAS OF **GRATITUDE**

TOP THREE **TO-DO'S** FOR TODAY

1. _____

2. _____

3. _____

DON'T **DOWNGRADE** YOUR **DREAM** JUST TO FIT YOUR **REALITY**. **UPGRADE** YOUR CONVICTION TO MATCH YOUR **DESTINY**.

Stuart Scott
Sportscaster and ESPN Anchor

TWO AREAS OF **GRATITUDE**

TOP THREE **TO-DO'S** FOR TODAY

1. _____
2. _____
3. _____

THE HAPPINESS OF YOUR **LIFE** DEPENDS UPON THE **QUALITY** OF YOUR **THOUGHTS**.

Marcus Aurelius
Emperor of Rome from 161 to 180

TWO AREAS OF **GRATITUDE**

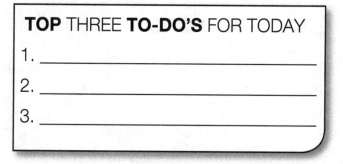

TOP THREE **TO-DO'S** FOR TODAY

1. _____
2. _____
3. _____

DON'T WAIT FOR
OPPORTUNITY.
CREATE IT.

Debasish Mridha, MD
Physicial, Philosopher, and Author

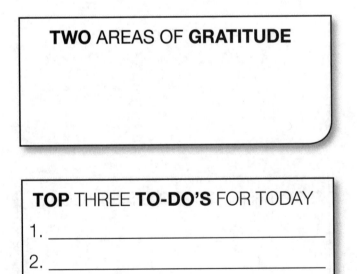

TWO AREAS OF **GRATITUDE**

TOP THREE **TO-DO'S** FOR TODAY

1. _____
2. _____
3. _____

EVERY MORNING YOU HAVE **TWO** CHOICES: CONTINUE TO **SLEEP** WITH YOUR **DREAMS**, OR **WAKE UP** AND **CHASE** THEM.

Unknown

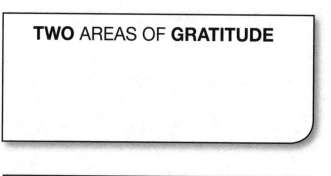

TWO AREAS OF **GRATITUDE**

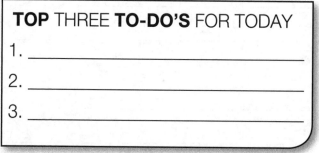

TOP THREE **TO-DO'S** FOR TODAY

1. _____

2. _____

3. _____

RANDOM **ACT** OF **KINDNESS**

SEND A **CARE** PACKAGE TO A **SOLDIER** OVERSEAS.

THOUGH **NO ONE** CAN GO BACK AND MAKE A BRAND-NEW START, **ANYONE** CAN **START** FROM **NOW** AND MAKE A BRAND-NEW **ENDING**.

Carl Bard
Author

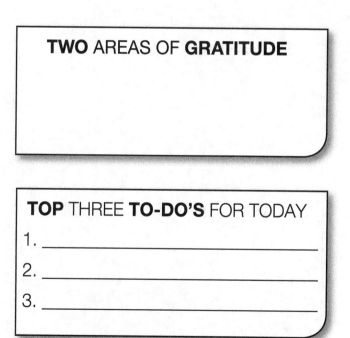

TWO AREAS OF **GRATITUDE**

TOP THREE **TO-DO'S** FOR TODAY

1. _____
2. _____
3. _____

WE MUST BE **WILLING** TO **LET GO** OF THE **LIFE** WE'VE **PLANNED** TO **HAVE** THE **LIFE** THAT IS **WAITING** FOR US.

Joseph Campbell
Mythologist, Author, and Lecturer

TWO AREAS OF **GRATITUDE**

TOP THREE **TO-DO'S** FOR TODAY

1. _____

2. _____

3. _____

SOMETIMES **LIFE** IS ABOUT RISKING EVERYTHING FOR A DREAM NO ONE CAN SEE **BUT YOU**.

Unknown

TWO AREAS OF **GRATITUDE**

TOP THREE **TO-DO'S** FOR TODAY

1. _____

2. _____

3. _____

DAY 95: DATE: _____

WE EITHER MAKE OURSELVES
MISERABLE
OR WE MAKE OURSELVES
STRONG.
THE AMOUNT OF WORK IS THE SAME.

Carlos Castaneda, PhD
Anthropology Author

TWO AREAS OF **GRATITUDE**

TOP THREE **TO-DO'S** FOR TODAY

1. _____
2. _____
3. _____

I REALIZED THIS WEEK THAT I JUST **CANNOT** DO IT ALL. SO I WILL **CHOOSE** TO DO WHAT **I CAN**, FABULOUSLY.

Clinton Kelly
Fashion Consultant and Co-Host of
What Not to Wear

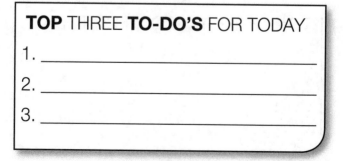

TWO AREAS OF **GRATITUDE**

TOP THREE **TO-DO'S** FOR TODAY

1. _____

2. _____

3. _____

DAY 97: DATE: _____

PEOPLE MAY **HEAR** YOUR WORDS, BUT THEY **FEEL** YOUR ATTITUDE.

John Maxwell
Author, Speaker, and Pastor

TWO AREAS OF **GRATITUDE**

TOP THREE **TO-DO'S** FOR TODAY

1. _____

2. _____

3. _____

STRENGTH
DOESN'T COME FROM
WHAT YOU **CAN DO**.
IT COMES FROM **OVERCOMING**
THE THINGS YOU
ONCE THOUGHT YOU **COULDN'T**.

Rikki Rogers
Graphic Designer

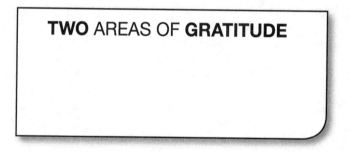

TWO AREAS OF **GRATITUDE**

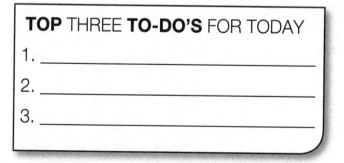

TOP THREE **TO-DO'S** FOR TODAY

1. _____

2. _____

3. _____

NOTES

NEVER ALLOW **WAITING** TO BECOME A **HABIT**. LIVE YOUR **DREAMS** AND TAKE **RISKS**. LIFE IS HAPPENING **NOW**.

Paulo Coelho
Brazilian Author

TWO AREAS OF **GRATITUDE**

TOP THREE **TO-DO'S** FOR TODAY

1. _____

2. _____

3. _____

STOP WAITING FOR FRIDAY, FOR **SUMMER**, FOR SOMEONE TO FALL IN **LOVE** WITH YOU, FOR **LIFE**. # HAPPINESS IS ACHIEVED WHEN YOU **STOP WAITING** FOR IT AND **MAKE THE MOST** OF THE MOMENT YOU ARE IN **NOW**.

Unknown

TWO AREAS OF **GRATITUDE**

TOP THREE **TO-DO'S** FOR TODAY

1. _____

2. _____

3. _____

BEING **POSITIVE**
IN A **NEGATIVE** SITUATION
IS NOT NAÏVE;
IT'S **LEADERSHIP.**

Ralph Marston
Former Professional Football Player

TWO AREAS OF **GRATITUDE**

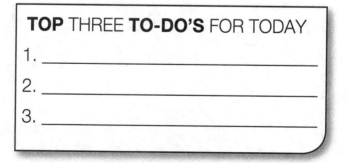

TOP THREE **TO-DO'S** FOR TODAY

1. _____

2. _____

3. _____

ONCE YOU **LEARN** TO BE HAPPY, YOU WON'T **TOLERATE** BEING AROUND **PEOPLE** WHO MAKE YOU FEEL ANYTHING LESS.

Unknown

TWO AREAS OF **GRATITUDE**

TOP THREE **TO-DO'S** FOR TODAY

1. _____

2. _____

3. _____

SUCCESS IS **NOT** THE KEY TO **HAPPINESS**. HAPPINESS IS THE KEY TO **SUCCESS**. IF YOU **LOVE** WHAT YOU ARE DOING, YOU WILL BE **SUCCESSFUL**.

Albert Schweitzer
French-German Theologian, Organist,
Philosopher, and Physician

TWO AREAS OF **GRATITUDE**

TOP THREE **TO-DO'S** FOR TODAY

1. _____

2. _____

3. _____

LOOK FOR SOMETHING
POSITIVE
IN EACH DAY,
EVEN IF SOME DAYS YOU HAVE TO
LOOK A LITTLE **HARDER**.

Unknown

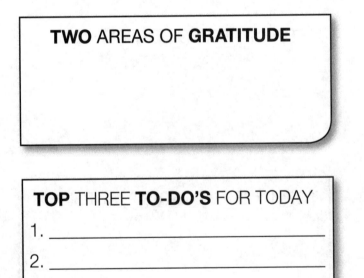

TWO AREAS OF **GRATITUDE**

TOP THREE **TO-DO'S** FOR TODAY

1. _____

2. _____

3. _____

THE **GREATEST** SOURCE OF HAPPINESS IS THE **ABILITY** TO BE GRATEFUL AT ALL TIMES.

Zig Ziglar
Motivational Speaker

TWO AREAS OF **GRATITUDE**

TOP THREE **TO-DO'S** FOR TODAY

1. _____
2. _____
3. _____

RANDOM **ACT** OF **KINDNESS**

TAKE TODAY TO **NOT COMPLAIN,** AND SEE HOW **GREAT** IT FEELS!

MY **GOAL** IS TO
BUILD A LIFE
I DON'T NEED A **VACATION** FROM!

Rob Hill, Sr.
Author, Entrepreneur, and Speaker

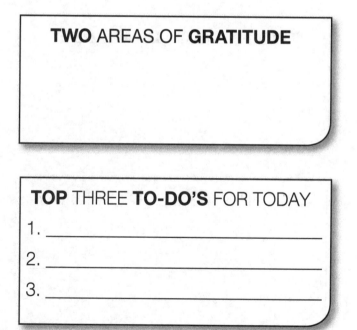

TWO AREAS OF **GRATITUDE**

TOP THREE **TO-DO'S** FOR TODAY

1. _____

2. _____

3. _____

YOU'LL **NEVER** CHANGE YOUR LIFE UNTIL YOU **CHANGE** SOMETHING YOU DO **DAILY**. THE **SECRET** OF YOUR SUCCESS IS FOUND IN YOUR **DAILY** ROUTINES.

John C. Maxwell
Author, Speaker, and Pastor

TWO AREAS OF **GRATITUDE**

TOP THREE **TO-DO'S** FOR TODAY

1. _____

2. _____

3. _____

MY MISSION: TO BE **SO BUSY** **LOVING** MY LIFE THAT I HAVE **NO TIME** FOR HATE, REGRET, WORRY, FRET, OR FEAR.

Loubis and Champagne
Quote Writer

TWO AREAS OF **GRATITUDE**

TOP THREE **TO-DO'S** FOR TODAY

1. _____

2. _____

3. _____

HOPE,
BUT NEVER **EXPECT**.
LOOK **FORWARD**,
BUT NEVER **WAIT**.

Unknown

TWO AREAS OF **GRATITUDE**

TOP THREE **TO-DO'S** FOR TODAY

1. _____
2. _____
3. _____

I AM **NOT**
WHAT **HAPPENED** TO ME;
I AM WHAT I **CHOOSE**
TO BECOME.

C. G. Jung
Swiss Founder of Analytical Psychology

TWO AREAS OF **GRATITUDE**

TOP THREE **TO-DO'S** FOR TODAY

1. _____
2. _____
3. _____

NEVER **BLAME** ANYONE IN YOUR LIFE. **GOOD** PEOPLE GIVE YOU **HAPPINESS**. **BAD** PEOPLE GIVE YOU **EXPERIENCE**. **WORST** PEOPLE GIVE YOU A **LESSON**, AND **BEST** PEOPLE GIVE YOU **MEMORIES**.

Unknown

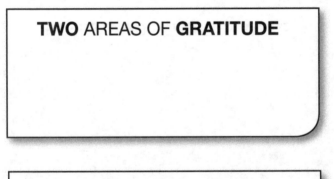

TWO AREAS OF **GRATITUDE**

TOP THREE **TO-DO'S** FOR TODAY

1. _____
2. _____
3. _____

AN **ARROW** CAN BE SHOT ONLY BY PULLING IT **BACKWARD**. SO WHEN **LIFE** IS **DRAGGING** YOU BACK WITH **DIFFICULTIES**, IT MEANS THAT IT'S GOING TO **LAUNCH** YOU INTO SOMETHING **GREAT**.

Unknown

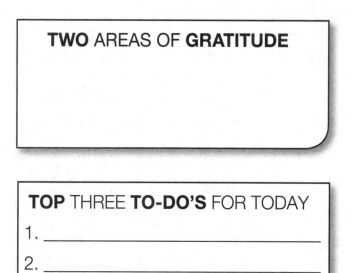

TWO AREAS OF **GRATITUDE**

TOP THREE **TO-DO'S** FOR TODAY

1. _____

2. _____

3. _____

NOTES

ENJOY THE **LITTLE THINGS** IN LIFE BECAUSE **ONE DAY** YOU WILL **LOOK BACK** AND REALIZE THEY WERE THE **BIG THINGS**.

Kurt Vonnegut
Writer

TWO AREAS OF **GRATITUDE**

TOP THREE **TO-DO'S** FOR TODAY

1. _____
2. _____
3. _____

YOU KNOW THE **FUTURE** IS **REALLY** HAPPENING WHEN YOU START FEELING **SCARED**.

Unknown

TWO AREAS OF **GRATITUDE**

TOP THREE **TO-DO'S** FOR TODAY

1. _____

2. _____

3. _____

WHEN SOMETHING **BAD** HAPPENS,
YOU HAVE **THREE** CHOICES:
YOU CAN EITHER
LET IT **DEFINE** YOU,
LET IT **DESTROY** YOU, OR
LET IT **STRENGTHEN** YOU.

Unknown

TWO AREAS OF **GRATITUDE**

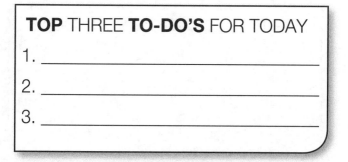

TOP THREE **TO-DO'S** FOR TODAY

1. _____

2. _____

3. _____

DAY 116: DATE: _____

RESPECT YOURSELF ENOUGH TO **WALK AWAY** FROM ANYTHING THAT NO LONGER **SERVES** YOU, **GROWS** YOU, OR MAKES YOU **HAPPY**.

Robert Tew
Writer

TWO AREAS OF **GRATITUDE**

TOP THREE **TO-DO'S** FOR TODAY

1. _____

2. _____

3. _____

THINGS THAT MATTER **MOST** MUST **NEVER** BE AT THE **MERCY** OF THINGS THAT MATTER **LEAST**.

Johann Wolfgang von Goethe
German Writer and Statesman

TWO AREAS OF **GRATITUDE**

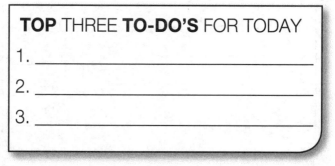

TOP THREE **TO-DO'S** FOR TODAY

1. _____
2. _____
3. _____

YOU ARE ALWAYS RESPONSIBLE FOR **HOW YOU ACT**, NO MATTER HOW YOU **FEEL**. REMEMBER THAT.

Robert Tew
Writer

TWO AREAS OF **GRATITUDE**

TOP THREE **TO-DO'S** FOR TODAY

1. _____
2. _____
3. _____

DON'T CONFUSE YOUR PATH WITH YOUR DESTINATION. JUST BECAUSE IT'S STORMY NOW DOESN'T MEAN THAT YOU AREN'T HEADED FOR SUNSHINE.

Unknown

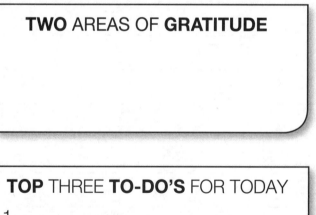

TWO AREAS OF **GRATITUDE**

TOP THREE **TO-DO'S** FOR TODAY

1. _____

2. _____

3. _____

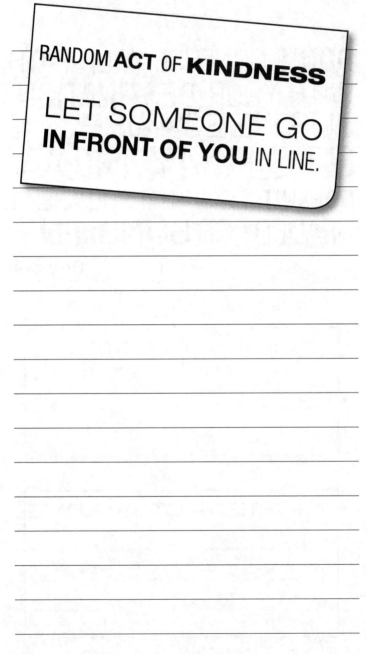

RANDOM **ACT** OF **KINDNESS**

LET SOMEONE GO **IN FRONT OF YOU** IN LINE.

A **GOOD LIFE** IS WHEN YOU SMILE OFTEN, DREAM **BIG**, **LAUGH** A LOT, AND REALIZE HOW **BLESSED** YOU ARE FOR WHAT YOU **HAVE**.

Unknown

TWO AREAS OF **GRATITUDE**

TOP THREE **TO-DO'S** FOR TODAY

1. _____

2. _____

3. _____

DREAM **BIG**, **WORK** HARD, STAY **FOCUSED**, AND **SURROUND** YOURSELF WITH **GOOD** PEOPLE.

Unknown

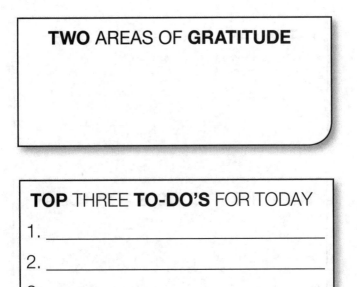

TWO AREAS OF **GRATITUDE**

TOP THREE **TO-DO'S** FOR TODAY

1. _____

2. _____

3. _____

THE **DISTANCE** BETWEEN YOUR **DREAMS** AND **REALITY** IS CALLED **ACTION**.

Unknown

TWO AREAS OF **GRATITUDE**

TOP THREE **TO-DO'S** FOR TODAY

1. _____
2. _____
3. _____

DON'T BE **ASHAMED** OF YOUR **STORY**. IT WILL **INSPIRE** OTHERS.

Unknown

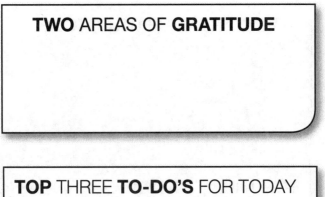

TWO AREAS OF **GRATITUDE**

TOP THREE **TO-DO'S** FOR TODAY

1. _____
2. _____
3. _____

FIRST, **THINK.**
SECOND, **BELIEVE.**
THIRD, **DREAM.** AND
FINALLY, **DARE.**

Walt Disney
Pioneer of the American Animation Industry

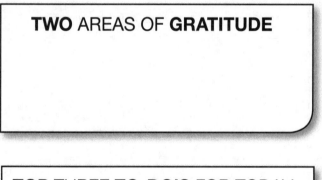

TWO AREAS OF **GRATITUDE**

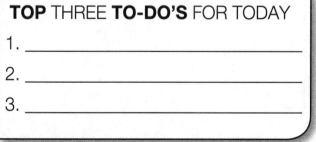

TOP THREE **TO-DO'S** FOR TODAY

1. _____
2. _____
3. _____

THE GREATEST **MISTAKE** YOU CAN MAKE IN **LIFE** IS TO CONTINUALLY **BE AFRAID** YOU WILL **MAKE ONE**.

Elbert Hubbard
Writer, Publisher, Artist, and Philosopher

TWO AREAS OF **GRATITUDE**

TOP THREE **TO-DO'S** FOR TODAY

1. _____

2. _____

3. _____

TODAY, GIVE YOURSELF **PERMISSION** TO BE OUTRAGEOUSLY **KIND**, IRRATIONALLY **WARM**, IMPROBABLY **GENEROUS**. I PROMISE, IT WILL BE A **BLAST**.

Sasha Dichter
Chief Innovation Officer, Acumen

TWO AREAS OF **GRATITUDE**

TOP THREE **TO-DO'S** FOR TODAY

1. _____

2. _____

3. _____

NOTES

DAY 127: DATE: _____

YOU ARE YOUR ONLY LIMIT.

Unknown

TWO AREAS OF **GRATITUDE**

TOP THREE **TO-DO'S** FOR TODAY

1. _____

2. _____

3. _____

IF YOU WANT **SOMETHING** YOU **NEVER** HAD, YOU HAVE TO **DO** SOMETHING YOU'VE **NEVER** DONE.

Thomas Jefferson
3rd US President

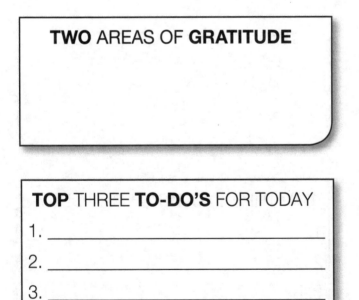

TWO AREAS OF **GRATITUDE**

TOP THREE **TO-DO'S** FOR TODAY

1. _____
2. _____
3. _____

PEOPLE WILL FORGET WHAT YOU **SAID**, PEOPLE WILL FORGET WHAT YOU **DID**, BUT PEOPLE WILL **NEVER** FORGET HOW YOU MADE THEM **FEEL**.

Maya Angelou
Poet, Memoirist, and Civil Rights Activist

TWO AREAS OF **GRATITUDE**

TOP THREE **TO-DO'S** FOR TODAY

1. _____

2. _____

3. _____

NOTHING CAN DIM THE **LIGHT** THAT **SHINES** FROM **WITHIN**.

Maya Angelou
Poet, Memoirist, and Civil Rights Activist

TWO AREAS OF **GRATITUDE**

TOP THREE **TO-DO'S** FOR TODAY

1. _____
2. _____
3. _____

YOU **DON'T** HAVE TO BE
PERFECT
TO BE **AMAZING.**

Unknown

TWO AREAS OF **GRATITUDE**

TOP THREE **TO-DO'S** FOR TODAY

1. _____

2. _____

3. _____

A LITTLE **PROGRESS** **EACH** DAY ADDS UP TO **BIG** RESULTS.

Unknown

TWO AREAS OF **GRATITUDE**

TOP THREE **TO-DO'S** FOR TODAY

1. _____
2. _____
3. _____

LET YOUR **SMILE CHANGE** THE WORLD, BUT **DON'T** LET THE **WORLD** CHANGE YOUR **SMILE**.

Unknown

TWO AREAS OF **GRATITUDE**

TOP THREE **TO-DO'S** FOR TODAY

1. _____
2. _____
3. _____

RANDOM **ACT** OF **KINDNESS**

GIVE A **STRANGER** A **COMPLIMENT**.

A **NEGATIVE** MIND WILL **NEVER** GIVE YOU A **POSITIVE LIFE**.

Ziad K. Abdelnour
Author

TWO AREAS OF **GRATITUDE**

TOP THREE **TO-DO'S** FOR TODAY

1. _____
2. _____
3. _____

FAILURE
IS A GREAT **TEACHER**,
AND, IF YOU'RE OPEN TO IT,
EVERY **MISTAKE**
HAS A **LESSON** TO OFFER.

Oprah Winfrey
Media Proprietor

TWO AREAS OF **GRATITUDE**

TOP THREE **TO-DO'S** FOR TODAY

1. _____

2. _____

3. _____

DON'T WAIT FOR EVERYTHING TO BE PERFECT BEFORE YOU DECIDE TO ENJOY YOUR LIFE.

Joyce Meyer
Charismatic Christian Author and Speaker

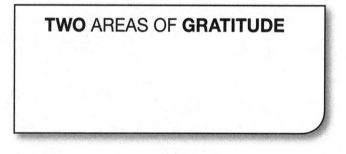

TWO AREAS OF **GRATITUDE**

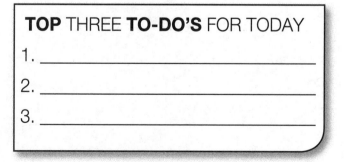

TOP THREE **TO-DO'S** FOR TODAY

1. _____
2. _____
3. _____

YOUR **VIBE** ATTRACTS YOUR **TRIBE.**

Unknown

TWO AREAS OF **GRATITUDE**

TOP THREE **TO-DO'S** FOR TODAY

1. _____

2. _____

3. _____

IF YOU **STUMBLE,** MAKE IT **PART** OF THE **DANCE.**

Unknown

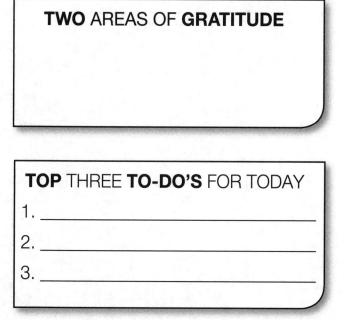

TWO AREAS OF **GRATITUDE**

TOP THREE **TO-DO'S** FOR TODAY

1. _____

2. _____

3. _____

LIFE IS **NOT** ABOUT **WAITING** FOR THE **STORM TO PASS,** BUT **LEARNING** TO **DANCE** IN THE RAIN.

Vivian Greene
Artist, Author, and Entrepreneur

TWO AREAS OF **GRATITUDE**

TOP THREE **TO-DO'S** FOR TODAY

1. _____
2. _____
3. _____

ALMOST EVERY **SUCCESSFUL PERSON** BEGINS WITH **TWO** BELIEFS: THE **FUTURE** CAN BE **BETTER** THAN THE PRESENT, AND I HAVE THE **POWER** TO **MAKE IT SO**.

David Brooks
Political and Cultural Commentator

TWO AREAS OF **GRATITUDE**

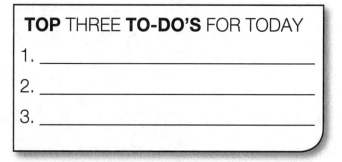

TOP THREE **TO-DO'S** FOR TODAY

1. _____
2. _____
3. _____

NOTES

BE **FEARLESS**
IN THE **PURSUIT** OF WHAT
SETS **YOUR SOUL** ON FIRE.

Unknown

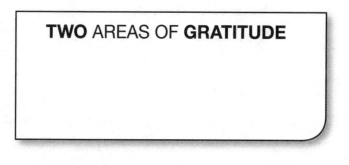

TWO AREAS OF **GRATITUDE**

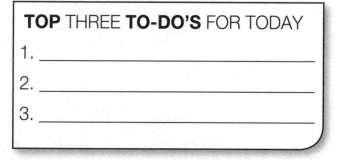

TOP THREE **TO-DO'S** FOR TODAY

1. _____
2. _____
3. _____

SHOOT FOR THE **MOON**. EVEN IF YOU **MISS**, YOU'LL **LAND** AMONG THE **STARS**.

Norman Vincent Peale
Minister and Author on Positive Thinking

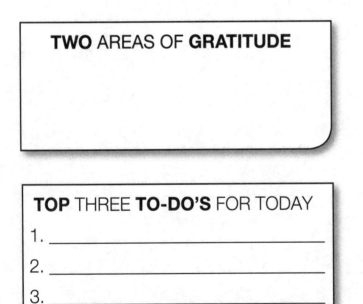

TWO AREAS OF **GRATITUDE**

TOP THREE **TO-DO'S** FOR TODAY

1. _____
2. _____
3. _____

THE **BEST** WAY TO GET THINGS **DONE** IS TO SIMPLY **BEGIN**.

Unknown

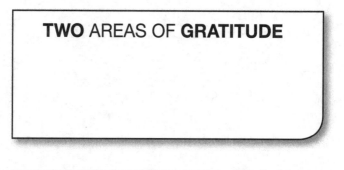

TWO AREAS OF **GRATITUDE**

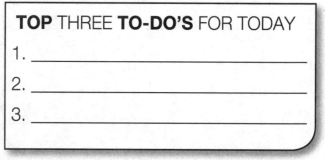

TOP THREE **TO-DO'S** FOR TODAY

1. _____

2. _____

3. _____

SOMETIMES THE SMALLEST STEP IN THE **RIGHT** DIRECTION ENDS UP BEING THE **BIGGEST** STEP OF YOUR LIFE. TIPTOE IF YOU MUST, BUT **TAKE THE STEP**.

Naeem Callaway
Founder and CEO of a Mentoring
Nonprofit for Kids

TWO AREAS OF **GRATITUDE**

TOP THREE **TO-DO'S** FOR TODAY

1. _____

2. _____

3. _____

SURROUND YOURSELF
WITH PEOPLE WHO REFLECT
WHO YOU **WANT TO BE**
AND **HOW** YOU **WANT TO FEEL**;
ENERGIES ARE
CONTAGIOUS.

Rachel Wolchin
Writer and Photographer

TWO AREAS OF **GRATITUDE**

TOP THREE **TO-DO'S** FOR TODAY

1. _____
2. _____
3. _____

NEVER GET **SO BUSY** MAKING A **LIVING** THAT YOU FORGET TO **MAKE A LIFE**.

Dolly Parton
Singer, Songwriter, and Actress

TWO AREAS OF **GRATITUDE**

TOP THREE **TO-DO'S** FOR TODAY

1. _____

2. _____

3. _____

ALWAYS GO WITH THE CHOICE THAT **SCARES** YOU **THE MOST** BECAUSE THAT'S **THE ONE** THAT IS GOING TO **HELP** YOU **GROW**.

Caroline Myss
Author

TWO AREAS OF **GRATITUDE**

TOP THREE **TO-DO'S** FOR TODAY

1. _____

2. _____

3. _____

RANDOM **ACT** OF **KINDNESS**

HOLD OPEN DOORS
FOR PEOPLE WHEREVER YOU GO.

FEAR HAS TWO MEANINGS: 'FORGET EVERYTHING AND RUN' OR 'FACE EVERYTHING AND RISE.' THE CHOICE IS YOURS.

Zig Ziglar
Motivational Speaker

TWO AREAS OF **GRATITUDE**

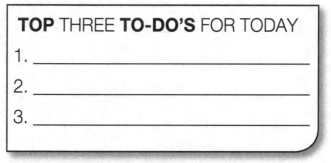

TOP THREE **TO-DO'S** FOR TODAY

1. _____

2. _____

3. _____

YOU ONLY LIVE **ONCE**. YOU **DON'T** WANT YOUR **TOMBSTONE** TO READ: **'PLAYED IT SAFE.'**

Rosario Dawson
Actress, Producer, and Comic Book Writer

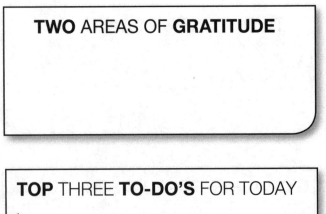

TWO AREAS OF **GRATITUDE**

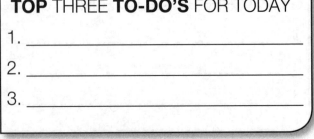

TOP THREE **TO-DO'S** FOR TODAY

1. _____
2. _____
3. _____

IT'S OKAY TO BE **SCARED.** BEING **SCARED** MEANS YOU'RE ABOUT TO DO **SOMETHING** REALLY, REALLY **BRAVE.**

Mandy Hale
Author and The Single Woman

TWO AREAS OF **GRATITUDE**

TOP THREE **TO-DO'S** FOR TODAY

1. _____
2. _____
3. _____

ALWAYS BELIEVE THAT
SOMETHING
WONDERFUL
IS ABOUT TO HAPPEN.

Unknown

TWO AREAS OF **GRATITUDE**

TOP THREE **TO-DO'S** FOR TODAY

1. _____
2. _____
3. _____

DOUBT KILLS MORE **DREAMS** THAN **FAILURE** EVER WILL.

Unknown

TWO AREAS OF **GRATITUDE**

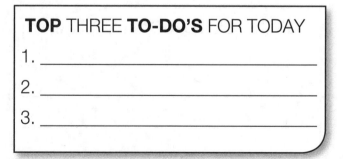

TOP THREE **TO-DO'S** FOR TODAY

1. _____

2. _____

3. _____

MAKING A **BIG** LIFE CHANGE IS PRETTY **SCARY**.
BUT YOU KNOW WHAT'S **EVEN SCARIER**?
REGRET.

Zig Ziglar
Motivational Speaker

TWO AREAS OF **GRATITUDE**

TOP THREE **TO-DO'S** FOR TODAY

1. _____

2. _____

3. _____

YOU HAD THE **POWER**
ALL ALONG, MY DEAR.

Glinda, The Good Witch
From *The Wizard of Oz*

TWO AREAS OF **GRATITUDE**

TOP THREE **TO-DO'S** FOR TODAY

1. _____

2. _____

3. _____

NOTES

DON'T GIVE UP.
GREAT THINGS TAKE **TIME**.
Unknown

TWO AREAS OF **GRATITUDE**

TOP THREE **TO-DO'S** FOR TODAY

1. _____

2. _____

3. _____

MAKE **TODAY** SO **AWESOME,** YESTERDAY GETS **JEALOUS.**

Unknown

TWO AREAS OF **GRATITUDE**

TOP THREE **TO-DO'S** FOR TODAY

1. _____
2. _____
3. _____

EITHER **YOU** RUN THE **DAY** OR THE **DAY RUNS YOU**.

Jim Rohn
Motivational Speaker and Author

TWO AREAS OF **GRATITUDE**

TOP THREE **TO-DO'S** FOR TODAY

1. _____

2. _____

3. _____

A **BAD** ATTITUDE IS LIKE A **FLAT TIRE**. YOU CAN'T GET VERY FAR UNTIL YOU **CHANGE IT**.

Unknown

TWO AREAS OF **GRATITUDE**

TOP THREE **TO-DO'S** FOR TODAY

1. _____

2. _____

3. _____

DON'T BE **AFRAID** TO **FAIL.**
BE AFRAID **NOT TO TRY**.

Unknown

TWO AREAS OF **GRATITUDE**

TOP THREE **TO-DO'S** FOR TODAY

1. _____

2. _____

3. _____

AT **ANY** GIVEN MOMENT, YOU HAVE THE **POWER** TO SAY: THIS IS **NOT** HOW THE STORY IS GOING TO **END**.

Christine Mason Miller
Author

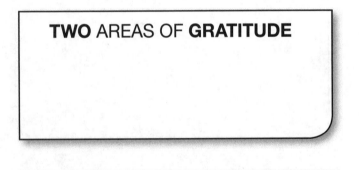

TWO AREAS OF **GRATITUDE**

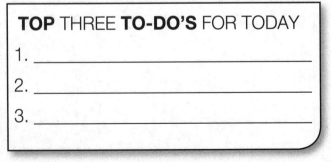

TOP THREE **TO-DO'S** FOR TODAY

1. _____
2. _____
3. _____

YOU'RE GIVEN ONLY ONE **LITTLE SPARK** OF **MADNESS.** YOU MUSTN'T **LOSE IT**.

Robin Williams
Stand-Up Comedian and Actor

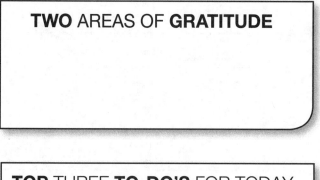

TWO AREAS OF **GRATITUDE**

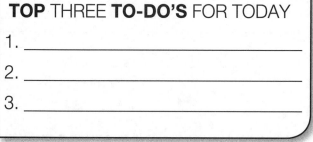

TOP THREE **TO-DO'S** FOR TODAY

1. _____

2. _____

3. _____

RANDOM **ACT** OF **KINDNESS**

DONATE YOUR OLD **CLOTHES** TO THE **SALVATION ARMY.**

DAY 162: DATE: _____

LIFE IS **10** PERCENT OF WHAT HAPPENS **TO YOU** AND **90** PERCENT HOW YOU **REACT** TO IT.

Charles R. Swindoll
Pastor, Author, Educator, and Radio Preacher

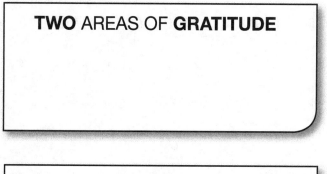

TWO AREAS OF **GRATITUDE**

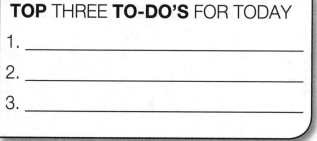

TOP THREE **TO-DO'S** FOR TODAY

1. _____
2. _____
3. _____

QUALITY
IS NOT AN **ACT**,
IT IS A **HABIT**.

Aristotle
Ancient Greek Philosopher and Scientist

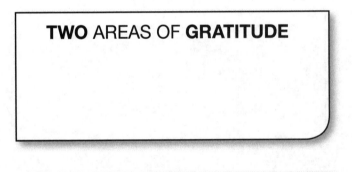

TWO AREAS OF **GRATITUDE**

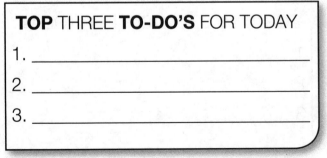

TOP THREE **TO-DO'S** FOR TODAY

1. _____

2. _____

3. _____

WITH THE **NEW** DAY COMES NEW **STRENGTH** AND NEW **THOUGHTS**.

Eleanor Roosevelt
Longest-Serving First Lady of the United States

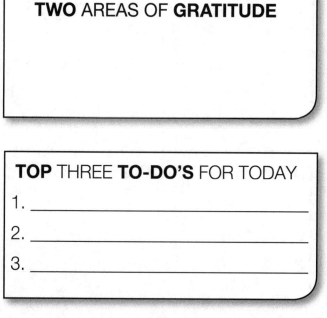

TWO AREAS OF **GRATITUDE**

TOP THREE **TO-DO'S** FOR TODAY

1. _____
2. _____
3. _____

IF YOU CAN **DREAM** IT, YOU CAN **DO IT**. ALWAYS REMEMBER, THIS **WHOLE** THING WAS STARTED BY A **MOUSE**.

Walt Disney
Pioneer of the American Animation Industry

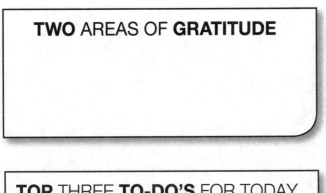

TWO AREAS OF **GRATITUDE**

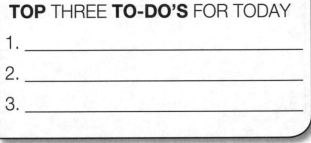

TOP THREE **TO-DO'S** FOR TODAY

1. _____
2. _____
3. _____

SETTING **GOALS** IS THE **FIRST STEP** IN TURNING THE INVISIBLE INTO THE **VISIBLE**.

Tony Robbins
Motivational Speaker and Change Catalyst

TWO AREAS OF **GRATITUDE**

TOP THREE **TO-DO'S** FOR TODAY

1. _____

2. _____

3. _____

TRUST **UNCERTAINTY** TO BRING YOU TO **CLARITY**.

Robert H. Schuller
Televangelist, Motivational Speaker, and Author

TWO AREAS OF **GRATITUDE**

TOP THREE **TO-DO'S** FOR TODAY

1. _____
2. _____
3. _____

KEEP YOUR **EYES** ON THE **STARS** AND YOUR **FEET** ON THE **GROUND**.

Theodore Roosevelt
26th US President

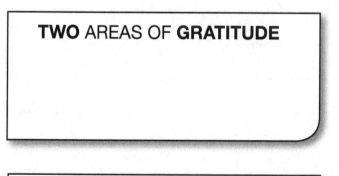

TWO AREAS OF **GRATITUDE**

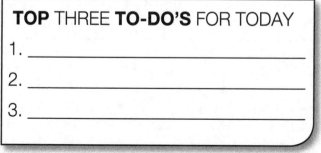

TOP THREE **TO-DO'S** FOR TODAY

1. _____
2. _____
3. _____

NOTES

KNOWING IS NOT ENOUGH; WE MUST **APPLY**. **WILLING** IS NOT ENOUGH; WE MUST **DO**.

Johann Wolfgang von Goethe
German Writer and Statesman

TWO AREAS OF **GRATITUDE**

TOP THREE **TO-DO'S** FOR TODAY

1. _____

2. _____

3. _____

NEVER, **NEVER,** **NEVER** GIVE UP.

Winston Churchill
Former Prime Minister of the United Kingdom

TWO AREAS OF **GRATITUDE**

TOP THREE **TO-DO'S** FOR TODAY

1. _____
2. _____
3. _____

WHEN SOMETHING IS IMPORTANT ENOUGH, **YOU DO IT** EVEN IF THE **ODDS** ARE **NOT** IN YOUR FAVOR.

Elon Musk
Business Magnate, Investor,
Engineer, and Inventor

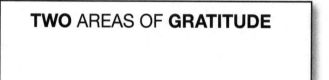

TWO AREAS OF **GRATITUDE**

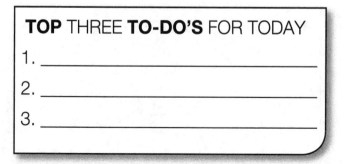

TOP THREE **TO-DO'S** FOR TODAY

1. _____

2. _____

3. _____

WELL DONE
IS **BETTER** THAN
WELL SAID.

Benjamin Franklin
Author, Printer, and Political Theorist

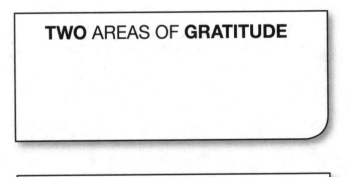

TWO AREAS OF **GRATITUDE**

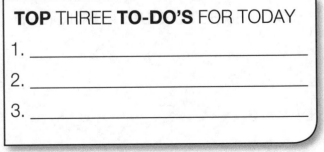

TOP THREE **TO-DO'S** FOR TODAY

1. _____

2. _____

3. _____

YOU ARE NEVER TOO OLD
TO SET ANOTHER **GOAL**
OR TO DREAM
A NEW DREAM.

C. S. Lewis
British Writer and Christian Apologist

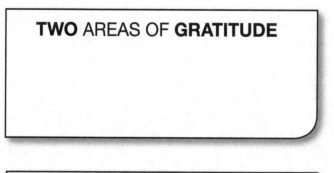

TWO AREAS OF **GRATITUDE**

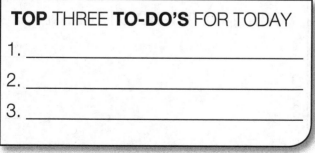

TOP THREE **TO-DO'S** FOR TODAY

1. _____
2. _____
3. _____

BE MISERABLE.
OR **MOTIVATE** YOURSELF.
WHATEVER HAS TO BE **DONE**,
IT'S ALWAYS YOUR **CHOICE**.

Wayne Dyer
Philosopher, Self-Help Author,
and Motivational Speaker

TWO AREAS OF **GRATITUDE**

TOP THREE **TO-DO'S** FOR TODAY

1. _____

2. _____

3. _____

GO FOR IT **NOW**. THE **FUTURE** IS PROMISED TO **NO ONE**.

Wayne Dyer
Philosopher, Self-Help Author,
and Motivational Speaker

TWO AREAS OF **GRATITUDE**

TOP THREE **TO-DO'S** FOR TODAY

1. _____

2. _____

3. _____

RANDOM **ACT** OF **KINDNESS**

SEND A **LETTER** TO A **GOOD** FRIEND INSTEAD OF A **TEXT.**

NEVER GIVE UP.
FOR THAT IS JUST THE **PLACE AND TIME** THAT THE TIDE WILL **TURN**.

Harriet Beecher Stowe
Abolitionist and Author

TWO AREAS OF **GRATITUDE**

TOP THREE **TO-DO'S** FOR TODAY

1. _____

2. _____

3. _____

SET YOUR GOALS **HIGH**, AND **DON'T STOP** TILL YOU GET THERE.

Bo Jackson

All-Star in Baseball and American Football

TWO AREAS OF **GRATITUDE**

TOP THREE **TO-DO'S** FOR TODAY

1. _____

2. _____

3. _____

IF YOU DON'T **LIKE** HOW THINGS ARE, **CHANGE IT!** YOU'RE NOT A **TREE.**

Jim Rohn
Entrepreneur, Author,
and Motivational Speaker

TWO AREAS OF **GRATITUDE**

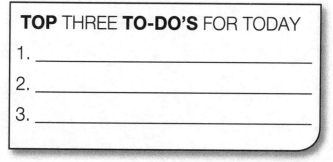

TOP THREE **TO-DO'S** FOR TODAY

1. _____
2. _____
3. _____

A **GOAL** IS A **DREAM** WITH A **DEADLINE.**

Napoleon Hill
Author of *Think and Grow Rich*

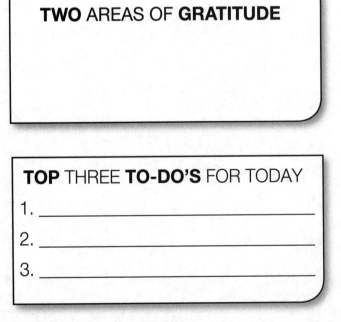

TWO AREAS OF **GRATITUDE**

TOP THREE **TO-DO'S** FOR TODAY

1. _____
2. _____
3. _____

PERSEVERANCE
IS **FAILING** 19 TIMES
AND **SUCCEEDING** THE 20TH.

Julie Andrews
English Actress, Singer, and Dancer

TWO AREAS OF **GRATITUDE**

TOP THREE **TO-DO'S** FOR TODAY

1. _____

2. _____

3. _____

TRUE HAPPINESS
INVOLVES THE FULL USE
OF ONE'S **POWER**
AND **TALENTS**.

John W. Gardner
Secretary of Health, Education, and Welfare
under President Lyndon Johnson

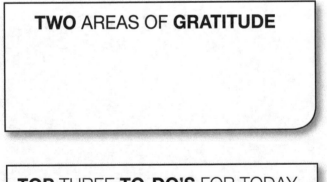

TWO AREAS OF **GRATITUDE**

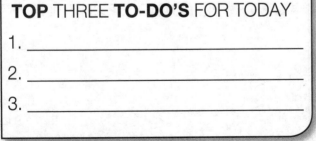

TOP THREE **TO-DO'S** FOR TODAY

1. _____
2. _____
3. _____

WHEREVER YOU ARE,
BE ALL THERE.

Jim Elliot
American Missionary Killed in Ecuador

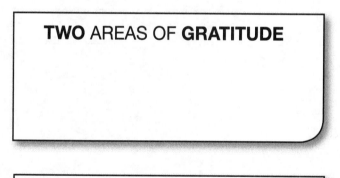

TWO AREAS OF **GRATITUDE**

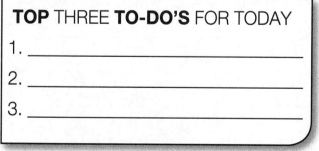

TOP THREE **TO-DO'S** FOR TODAY

1. _____

2. _____

3. _____

NOTES

I DON'T **BELIEVE** YOU HAVE TO BE **BETTER** THAN ANYONE ELSE. I **BELIEVE** YOU HAVE TO BE **BETTER THAN** YOU EVER **THOUGHT YOU COULD BE.**

Ken Venturi
Professional Golfer and Golf Broadcaster

TWO AREAS OF **GRATITUDE**

TOP THREE **TO-DO'S** FOR TODAY

1. _____

2. _____

3. _____

ONE FINDS **LIMITS** BY **PUSHING** THEM.

Herbert Simon
Economist, Sociologist, Psychologist, and
Computer Scientist

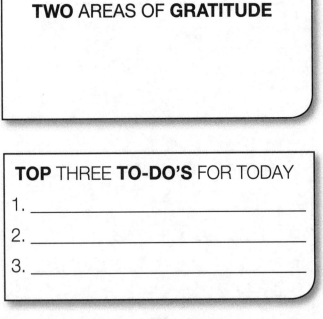

TWO AREAS OF **GRATITUDE**

TOP THREE **TO-DO'S** FOR TODAY

1. _____

2. _____

3. _____

DO NOT WAIT; THE TIME WILL NEVER BE 'JUST RIGHT.' START WHERE YOU STAND, AND WORK WITH WHATEVER TOOLS YOU MAY HAVE AT YOUR COMMAND, AND BETTER TOOLS WILL BE FOUND AS YOU GO ALONG.

Albert Schweitzer
French-German Theologian, Organist,
Philosopher, and Physician

TWO AREAS OF **GRATITUDE**

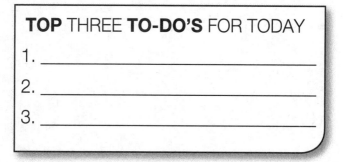

TOP THREE **TO-DO'S** FOR TODAY

1. _____

2. _____

3. _____

THE **PEOPLE** WHO **INFLUENCE** YOU ARE THE **PEOPLE** WHO **BELIEVE** IN YOU.

Henry Drummond
Scottish Evangelist, Biologist, Writer, and Lecturer

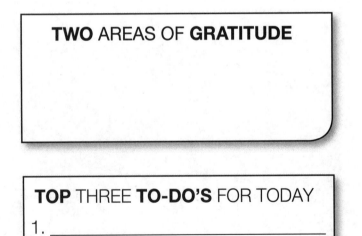

TWO AREAS OF **GRATITUDE**

TOP THREE **TO-DO'S** FOR TODAY

1. _____

2. _____

3. _____

THE BEST **PREPARATION** FOR **TOMORROW** IS DOING YOUR BEST **TODAY.**

H. Jackson Brown, Jr.
Author of *Life's Little Instruction Book*

TWO AREAS OF **GRATITUDE**

TOP THREE **TO-DO'S** FOR TODAY

1. _____

2. _____

3. _____

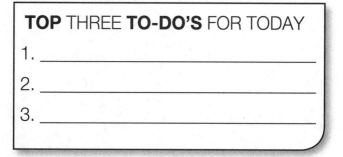

NOTHING IS **IMPOSSIBLE;** THE WORD ITSELF SAYS **"I'M POSSIBLE."**

Audrey Hepburn
British Actress, Model, Dancer, and Humanitarian

TWO AREAS OF **GRATITUDE**

TOP THREE **TO-DO'S** FOR TODAY

1. _____
2. _____
3. _____

WHAT LIES **BEHIND** YOU AND WHAT LIES IN **FRONT** OF YOU PALE IN COMPARISON TO WHAT LIES **WITHIN** YOU.

Ralph Waldo Emerson
Essayist, Lecturer, and Poet

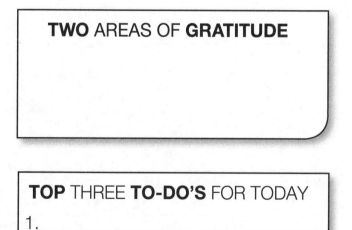

TWO AREAS OF **GRATITUDE**

TOP THREE **TO-DO'S** FOR TODAY

1. _____

2. _____

3. _____

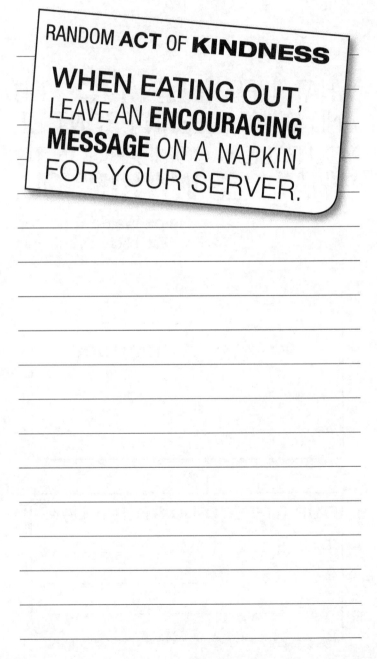

RANDOM **ACT** OF **KINDNESS**

WHEN EATING OUT, LEAVE AN **ENCOURAGING MESSAGE** ON A NAPKIN FOR YOUR SERVER.

WHAT WE **THINK**, **WE BECOME.**

Buddha
Nepalese Ascetic and Sage

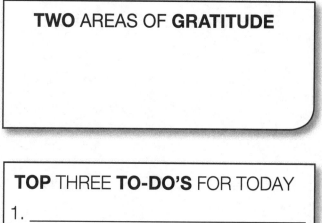

TWO AREAS OF **GRATITUDE**

TOP THREE **TO-DO'S** FOR TODAY

1. _____
2. _____
3. _____

KEEP YOUR FACE ALWAYS
TOWARD THE SUNSHINE,
AND **SHADOWS** WILL
FALL BEHIND YOU.

Walt Whitman
Poet, Essayist, and Journalist

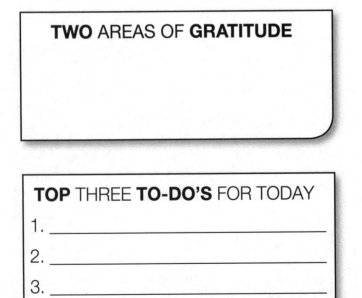

TWO AREAS OF **GRATITUDE**

TOP THREE **TO-DO'S** FOR TODAY

1. _____

2. _____

3. _____

IT IS **NEVER** TOO LATE **TO BE** WHAT YOU MIGHT HAVE BEEN.

George Elliot
American Missionary Killed in Ecuador

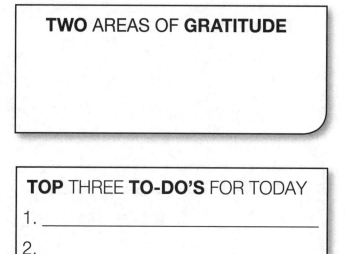

TWO AREAS OF **GRATITUDE**

TOP THREE **TO-DO'S** FOR TODAY

1. _____

2. _____

3. _____

CHANGE YOUR **THOUGHTS**, AND **YOU CHANGE** YOUR **WORLD**.

Norman Vincent Peale
Minister and Author on Positive Thinking

TWO AREAS OF **GRATITUDE**

TOP THREE **TO-DO'S** FOR TODAY

1. _____
2. _____
3. _____

NO ACT OF **KINDNESS**, NO MATTER HOW SMALL, IS EVER **WASTED**.

Aesop
Greek Fabulist and Story Teller

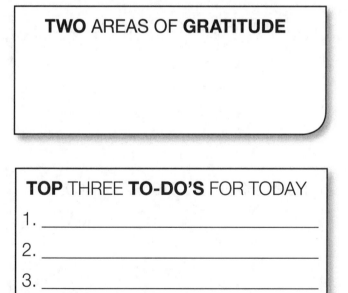

TWO AREAS OF **GRATITUDE**

TOP THREE **TO-DO'S** FOR TODAY

1. _____

2. _____

3. _____

A **HERO** IS SOMEONE WHO HAS **GIVEN** HIS OR HER **LIFE** TO SOMETHING **BIGGER** THAN ONESELF.

Joseph Campbell
Mythologist, Author, and Lecturer

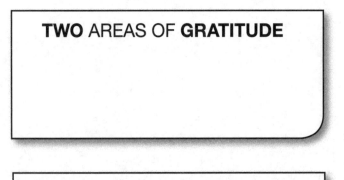

TWO AREAS OF **GRATITUDE**

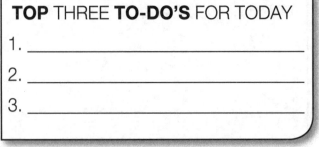

TOP THREE **TO-DO'S** FOR TODAY

1. _____

2. _____

3. _____

WE CAN'T HELP EVERYONE, BUT **EVERYONE** CAN HELP SOMEONE.

Ronald Reagan
40th US President

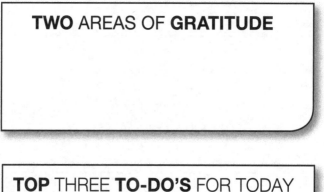

TWO AREAS OF **GRATITUDE**

TOP THREE **TO-DO'S** FOR TODAY

1. _____
2. _____
3. _____

NOTES

START BY DOING WHAT'S NECESSARY, THEN DO WHAT'S POSSIBLE, AND SUDDENLY YOU ARE DOING THE IMPOSSIBLE.

Francis of Assisi
Italian Roman Catholic Friar, Deacon,
and Preacher

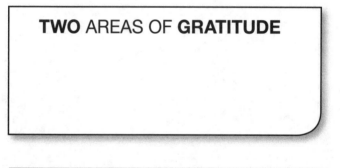

TWO AREAS OF **GRATITUDE**

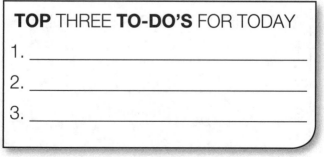

TOP THREE **TO-DO'S** FOR TODAY

1. _____
2. _____
3. _____

IT IS IN YOUR **MOMENTS OF DECISION** THAT YOUR **DESTINY IS SHAPED.**

Tony Robbins
Motivational Speaker and Change Catalyst

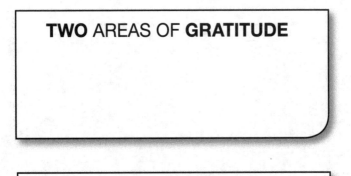

TWO AREAS OF **GRATITUDE**

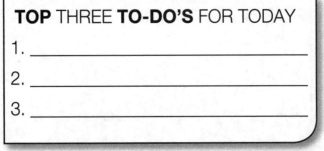

TOP THREE **TO-DO'S** FOR TODAY

1. _____
2. _____
3. _____

YOU MUST **DO** THE THINGS YOU **THINK** YOU **CANNOT DO.**

Eleanor Roosevelt
Longest-Serving First Lady of the United States

TWO AREAS OF **GRATITUDE**

TOP THREE **TO-DO'S** FOR TODAY

1. _____
2. _____
3. _____

WHEN WE **SEEK** TO DISCOVER THE **BEST** IN OTHERS, WE SOMETIMES BRING OUT THE **BEST** IN OURSELVES.

William Arthur Ward
Inspirational Writer

TWO AREAS OF **GRATITUDE**

TOP THREE **TO-DO'S** FOR TODAY

1. _____

2. _____

3. _____

ALL YOU NEED IS **THE PLAN**, THE ROAD MAP, AND THE **COURAGE** TO **PRESS ON** TO YOUR **DESTINATION**.

Earl Nightingale
Radio Personality and Author on Human
Character Development

TWO AREAS OF **GRATITUDE**

TOP THREE **TO-DO'S** FOR TODAY

1. _____

2. _____

3. _____

YOUR BIG **OPPORTUNITY** MAY BE **RIGHT** WHERE **YOU ARE NOW.**

Napoleon Hill
Author of *Think and Grow Rich*

TWO AREAS OF **GRATITUDE**

TOP THREE **TO-DO'S** FOR TODAY

1. _____

2. _____

3. _____

FIND OUT **WHO YOU ARE**, AND BE THAT PERSON. THAT'S WHAT **YOUR SOUL** WAS PUT ON THIS EARTH TO BE. **FIND** THAT TRUTH, **LIVE** THAT **TRUTH**, AND EVERYTHING ELSE WILL COME.

Ellen DeGeneres
Comedienne, TV Host, and Producer

TWO AREAS OF **GRATITUDE**

TOP THREE **TO-DO'S** FOR TODAY

1. _____

2. _____

3. _____

RANDOM **ACT** OF **KINDNESS**

TAKE THE TIME TO
APPRECIATE
THE SUNRISE AND SUNSET.

LIVE YOUR BELIEFS, AND YOU CAN TURN THIS WORLD AROUND.

Henry David Thoreau
Essayist, Poet, and Philosopher

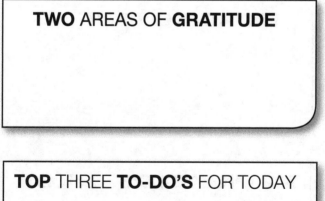

TWO AREAS OF **GRATITUDE**

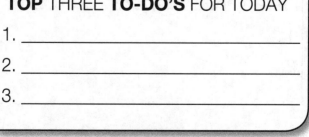

TOP THREE **TO-DO'S** FOR TODAY

1. _____

2. _____

3. _____

FROM WHAT WE **GET**, WE CAN **MAKE A LIVING**; WHAT WE **GIVE**, HOWEVER, **MAKES A LIFE.**

Arthur Ashe
American World No. 1 Professional Tennis Player

TWO AREAS OF **GRATITUDE**

TOP THREE **TO-DO'S** FOR TODAY

1. _____

2. _____

3. _____

IF WE **DID** ALL THE THINGS WE WERE **CAPABLE** OF, WE WOULD LITERALLY **ASTOUND OURSELVES.**

Thomas Edison
Inventor and Businessman

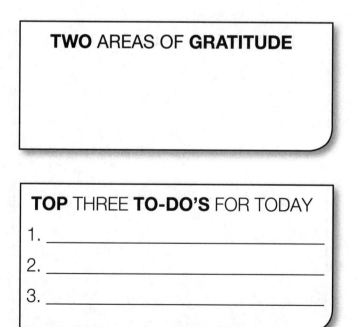

TWO AREAS OF **GRATITUDE**

TOP THREE **TO-DO'S** FOR TODAY

1. _____
2. _____
3. _____

KEEP ALL SPECIAL **THOUGHTS** AND **MEMORIES** FOR LIFETIMES TO COME. **SHARE** THESE KEEPSAKES WITH OTHERS TO **INSPIRE HOPE** AND BUILD FROM THE **PAST**, WHICH CAN BRIDGE TO THE **FUTURE**.

Mattie Stepanek
Teenage Poet and Peace Advocate

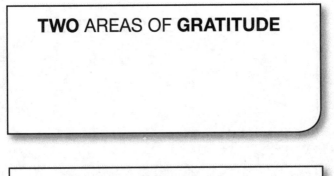

TWO AREAS OF **GRATITUDE**

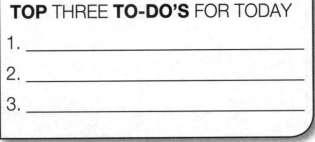

TOP THREE **TO-DO'S** FOR TODAY

1. _____
2. _____
3. _____

WHAT WE NEED IS **MORE PEOPLE** WHO **SPECIALIZE** IN THE **IMPOSSIBLE.**

Theodore Roethke
Poet

TWO AREAS OF **GRATITUDE**

TOP THREE **TO-DO'S** FOR TODAY

1. _____
2. _____
3. _____

AS **KNOWLEDGE** INCREASES, **WONDER** DEEPENS.

Charles Morgan
Railroad and Shipping Magnate

TWO AREAS OF **GRATITUDE**

TOP THREE **TO-DO'S** FOR TODAY

1. _____

2. _____

3. _____

A PLACE FOR EVERYTHING,
EVERYTHING IN ITS PLACE.

Benjamin Franklin
Author, Printer, and Political Theorist

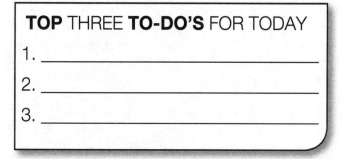

TWO AREAS OF **GRATITUDE**

TOP THREE **TO-DO'S** FOR TODAY

1. _____
2. _____
3. _____

NOTES

YOUR PRESENT CIRCUMSTANCES DON'T DETERMINE WHERE YOU CAN GO; THEY MERELY **DETERMINE** WHERE YOU **START**.

Nido Qubein
President of High Point University

TWO AREAS OF **GRATITUDE**

TOP THREE **TO-DO'S** FOR TODAY

1. _____
2. _____
3. _____

WHEN YOU HAVE A **DREAM**, YOU'VE GOT TO **GRAB IT** AND **NEVER LET GO**.

Carol Burnett
Actress, Comedienne, Singer, and Writer

TWO AREAS OF **GRATITUDE**

TOP THREE **TO-DO'S** FOR TODAY

1. _____
2. _____
3. _____

WHAT **GREAT** THING WOULD YOU ATTEMPT IF YOU KNEW YOU COULD **NOT FAIL**?

Robert H. Schuller
Televangelist, Motivational Speaker, and Author

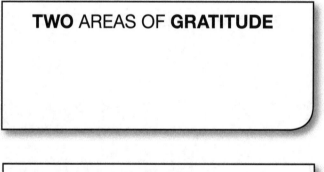

TWO AREAS OF **GRATITUDE**

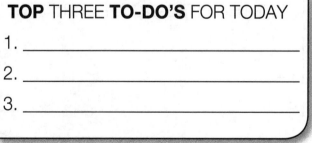

TOP THREE **TO-DO'S** FOR TODAY

1. _____

2. _____

3. _____

THE BEST WAY **OUT** IS ALWAYS **THROUGH**.

Robert Frost
Poet

TWO AREAS OF **GRATITUDE**

TOP THREE **TO-DO'S** FOR TODAY

1. _____

2. _____

3. _____

WE CAN **CHANGE OUR LIVES.**
WE CAN **DO, HAVE,** AND **BE**
EXACTLY WHAT WE **WISH.**

Tony Robbins
Motivational Speaker and Change Catalyst

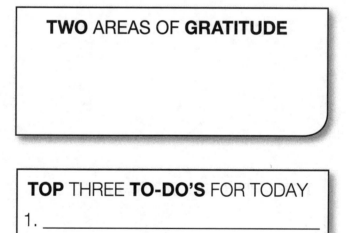

TWO AREAS OF **GRATITUDE**

TOP THREE **TO-DO'S** FOR TODAY

1. _____

2. _____

3. _____

EVEN IF YOU'RE ON **THE RIGHT TRACK,** YOU'LL GET **RUN OVER** IF YOU JUST **SIT THERE.**

Will Rogers
Actor, Humorist, Columnist,
and Social Commentator

TWO AREAS OF **GRATITUDE**

TOP THREE **TO-DO'S** FOR TODAY

1. _____

2. _____

3. _____

WHEN I HEAR SOMEBODY SIGH, 'LIFE IS HARD,' I'M ALWAYS TEMPTED TO ASK, 'COMPARED TO WHAT?'

Sydney Harris
Journalist

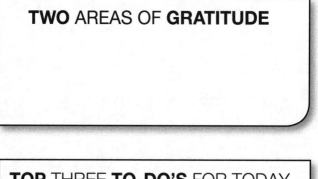

TWO AREAS OF **GRATITUDE**

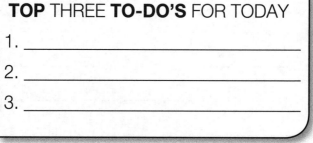

TOP THREE **TO-DO'S** FOR TODAY

1. _____
2. _____
3. _____

RANDOM **ACT** OF **KINDNESS**

HIDE MONEY IN A **RANDOM PLACE** FOR A **STRANGER** TO FIND.

WHEN I **LET GO** OF WHAT I AM, **I BECOME** WHAT I **MIGHT BE**.

Lao Tzu
Ancient Chinese Philosopher

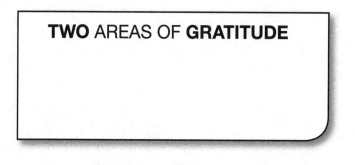

TWO AREAS OF **GRATITUDE**

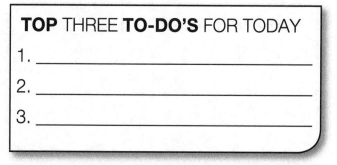

TOP THREE **TO-DO'S** FOR TODAY

1. _____

2. _____

3. _____

COURAGE IS THE **FIRST** OF HUMAN QUALITIES BECAUSE IT IS THE **QUALITY** WHICH **GUARANTEES** ALL OTHERS.

Winston Churchill
Former Prime Minister of the United Kingdom

TWO AREAS OF **GRATITUDE**

TOP THREE **TO-DO'S** FOR TODAY

1. _____
2. _____
3. _____

THE **DIFFERENCE** BETWEEN A **SUCCESSFUL** PERSON AND OTHERS IS **NOT** A LACK OF **STRENGTH** AND **NOT** A LACK OF **KNOWLEDGE** BUT RATHER A **LACK OF WILL**.

Vince Lombardi
Former American Football Player,
Coach, and NFL Executive

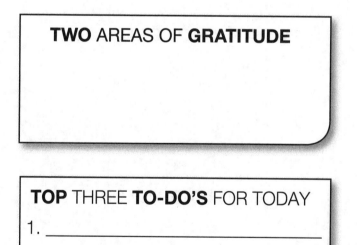

TWO AREAS OF **GRATITUDE**

TOP THREE **TO-DO'S** FOR TODAY

1. _____
2. _____
3. _____

DON'T WORRY ABOUT FAILURES. WORRY ABOUT THE CHANCES YOU MISS WHEN YOU DON'T EVEN TRY.

Jack Canfield
Author, Motivational Speaker,
and Corporate Trainer

TWO AREAS OF **GRATITUDE**

TOP THREE **TO-DO'S** FOR TODAY

1. _____

2. _____

3. _____

SOME MEN SEE THINGS **AS THEY ARE** AND SAY **WHY**. I DREAM THINGS THAT **NEVER WERE** AND SAY **WHY NOT**.

George Bernard Shaw
Irish Playwright

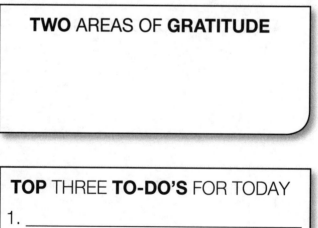

TWO AREAS OF **GRATITUDE**

TOP THREE **TO-DO'S** FOR TODAY

1. _____

2. _____

3. _____

SPEAK LESS
THAN YOU **KNOW;**
HAVE MORE THAN YOU **SHOW**.

William Shakespeare
English Poet, Playwright, and Actor

TWO AREAS OF **GRATITUDE**

TOP THREE **TO-DO'S** FOR TODAY

1. _____

2. _____

3. _____

THE **JOURNEY** OF A THOUSAND MILES BEGINS WITH **ONE STEP**.

Lao Tzu
Ancient Chinese Philosopher

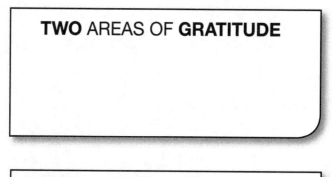

TWO AREAS OF **GRATITUDE**

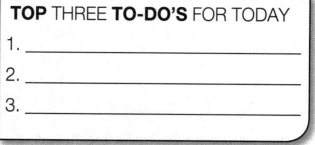

TOP THREE **TO-DO'S** FOR TODAY

1. _____

2. _____

3. _____

NOTES

DO NOT LET WHAT YOU CANNOT DO INTERFERE WITH WHAT YOU CAN DO.

John Wooden
Basketball Player and UCLA Head Coach

TWO AREAS OF **GRATITUDE**

TOP THREE **TO-DO'S** FOR TODAY

1. _____
2. _____
3. _____

CHALLENGES
ARE WHAT MAKE LIFE
INTERESTING,
AND **OVERCOMING** THEM
IS WHAT MAKES LIFE
MEANINGFUL.

Joshua J. Marine
Author

TWO AREAS OF **GRATITUDE**

TOP THREE **TO-DO'S** FOR TODAY

1. _____

2. _____

3. _____

AN **OBSTACLE** IS OFTEN A **STEPPING STONE**.

William Prescott
American Colonel in the Revolutionary War

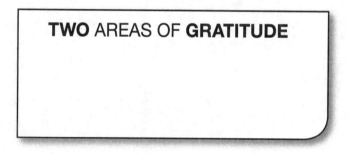

TWO AREAS OF **GRATITUDE**

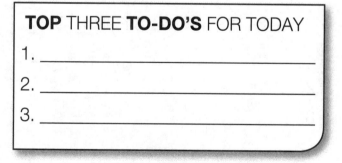

TOP THREE **TO-DO'S** FOR TODAY

1. _____

2. _____

3. _____

I **AM NOT** A PRODUCT OF MY **CIRCUMSTANCES.** I **AM** A PRODUCT OF MY **DECISIONS.**

Stephen Covey
Educator, Author, and Keynote Speaker

TWO AREAS OF **GRATITUDE**

TOP THREE **TO-DO'S** FOR TODAY

1. _____
2. _____
3. _____

KEEP AWAY FROM PEOPLE WHO TRY TO **BELITTLE** YOUR **AMBITIONS**. **SMALL PEOPLE** ALWAYS DO THAT, BUT THE REALLY **GREAT** PERSON MAKES YOU FEEL THAT **YOU, TOO, CAN BECOME GREAT**.

Mark Twain
Writer

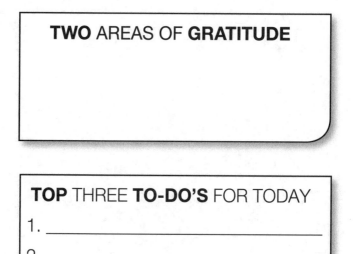

TWO AREAS OF **GRATITUDE**

TOP THREE **TO-DO'S** FOR TODAY

1. _____
2. _____
3. _____

I AM **THANKFUL** FOR ALL OF THOSE WHO SAID **NO** TO ME. IT'S BECAUSE OF THEM **I'M DOING IT MYSELF.**

Albert Einstein
Theoretical Physicist

TWO AREAS OF **GRATITUDE**

TOP THREE **TO-DO'S** FOR TODAY

1. _____

2. _____

3. _____

THE PESSIMIST
SEES **DIFFICULTY** IN EVERY
OPPORTUNITY.
THE OPTIMIST
SEES THE **OPPORTUNITY**
IN EVERY DIFFICULTY.

Winston Churchill
Former Prime Minister of the United Kingdom

TWO AREAS OF **GRATITUDE**

TOP THREE **TO-DO'S** FOR TODAY

1. _____

2. _____

3. _____

RANDOM **ACT** OF **KINDNESS**

RECONNECT
WITH AN OLD FRIEND.

IT'S **NOT** WHETHER YOU **GET KNOCKED DOWN;** IT'S WHETHER YOU **GET UP**.

Vince Lombardi
Former American Football Player, Coach,
and NFL Executive

TWO AREAS OF **GRATITUDE**

TOP THREE **TO-DO'S** FOR TODAY

1. _____

2. _____

3. _____

IF YOU ARE WORKING ON SOMETHING **EXCITING** THAT YOU **REALLY CARE** ABOUT, YOU **DON'T** HAVE TO BE **PUSHED**. THE VISION **PULLS** YOU.

Steve Jobs
Cofounder, Chairman, and CEO, Apple Inc.

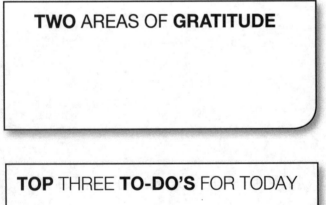

TWO AREAS OF **GRATITUDE**

TOP THREE **TO-DO'S** FOR TODAY

1. _____

2. _____

3. _____

WE MAY ENCOUNTER **MANY DEFEATS,** BUT WE MUST **NEVER** BE **DEFEATED**.

Maya Angelou
Poet, Memoirist, and Civil Rights Activist

TWO AREAS OF **GRATITUDE**

TOP THREE **TO-DO'S** FOR TODAY

1. _____

2. _____

3. _____

WE GENERATE **FEARS** WHILE WE **SIT**. WE **OVERCOME** THEM BY **ACTION**.

Dr. Henry Link

TWO AREAS OF **GRATITUDE**

TOP THREE **TO-DO'S** FOR TODAY

1. _____
2. _____
3. _____

WHETHER YOU THINK YOU **CAN** OR THINK YOU **CAN'T**, **YOU'RE RIGHT**.

Henry Ford
Industrialist and Founder of the
Ford Motor Company

TWO AREAS OF **GRATITUDE**

TOP THREE **TO-DO'S** FOR TODAY

1. _____
2. _____
3. _____

SECURITY IS MOSTLY A SUPERSTITION. LIFE IS EITHER A DARING ADVENTURE OR NOTHING.

Helen Keller
Writer and Political Activist

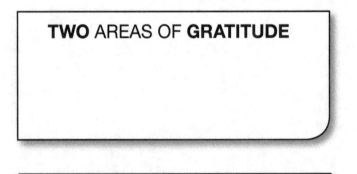

TWO AREAS OF **GRATITUDE**

TOP THREE **TO-DO'S** FOR TODAY

1. _____

2. _____

3. _____

THE MAN WHO HAS CONFIDENCE IN HIMSELF GAINS THE **CONFIDENCE OF OTHERS.**

Hasidic Proverb

TWO AREAS OF **GRATITUDE**

TOP THREE **TO-DO'S** FOR TODAY

1. _____

2. _____

3. _____

NOTES

CREATIVITY IS INTELLIGENCE **HAVING FUN.**

Albert Einstein
Theoretical Physicist

TWO AREAS OF **GRATITUDE**

TOP THREE **TO-DO'S** FOR TODAY

1. _____

2. _____

3. _____

DO WHAT YOU CAN
WITH **ALL** YOU HAVE,
WHEREVER YOU ARE.

Theodore Roosevelt
26th US President

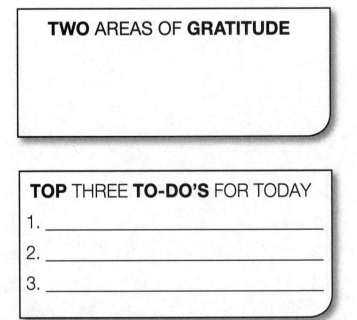

TWO AREAS OF **GRATITUDE**

TOP THREE **TO-DO'S** FOR TODAY

1. _____

2. _____

3. _____

DEVELOP AN '**ATTITUDE** OF **GRATITUDE**.' SAY **THANK YOU** TO EVERYONE YOU MEET **FOR EVERYTHING** THEY DO FOR YOU.

Brian Tracy
Motivational Public Speaker and
Self-Development Author

TWO AREAS OF **GRATITUDE**

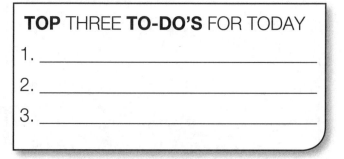

TOP THREE **TO-DO'S** FOR TODAY

1. _____
2. _____
3. _____

WHATEVER THE MIND OF MAN CAN **CONCEIVE** AND **BELIEVE,** IT CAN **ACHIEVE.**

Napoleon Hill
Author of *Think and Grow Rich*

TWO AREAS OF **GRATITUDE**

TOP THREE **TO-DO'S** FOR TODAY

1. _____
2. _____
3. _____

YOU **MISS** 100 PERCENT OF THE **SHOTS** YOU DON'T TAKE.

Wayne Gretzky
Canadian Former Professional Ice Hockey Player

TWO AREAS OF **GRATITUDE**

TOP THREE **TO-DO'S** FOR TODAY

1. _____

2. _____

3. _____

I'VE **MISSED** MORE THAN 9,000 SHOTS IN MY CAREER. I'VE **LOST** ALMOST **300** GAMES. TWENTY-SIX TIMES I'VE BEEN TRUSTED TO TAKE THE GAME-WINNING SHOT **AND MISSED. I'VE FAILED** OVER AND OVER AND OVER AGAIN IN MY LIFE. AND **THAT IS WHY I SUCCEED**.

Michael Jordan
Retired Professional Basketball Player

TWO AREAS OF **GRATITUDE**

TOP THREE **TO-DO'S** FOR TODAY

1. _____

2. _____

3. _____

DEFINITENESS OF PURPOSE
IS THE **STARTING POINT** OF ALL **ACHIEVEMENT**.

W. Clement Stone
Businessman, Philanthropist, and
New Thought Self-Help Book Author

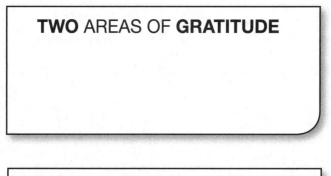

TWO AREAS OF **GRATITUDE**

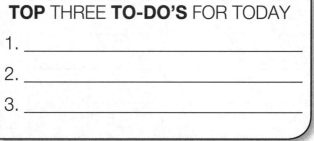

TOP THREE **TO-DO'S** FOR TODAY

1. _____

2. _____

3. _____

RANDOM **ACT** OF **KINDNESS**

DELIVER **TREATS** TO SOMEONE WHO COULD USE A **PICK-ME-UP**.

LIFE IS WHAT HAPPENS
TO YOU WHEN YOU'RE BUSY MAKING OTHER PLANS.

John Lennon
Cofounder of The Beatles

TWO AREAS OF **GRATITUDE**

TOP THREE **TO-DO'S** FOR TODAY

1. _____

2. _____

3. _____

TWENTY YEARS FROM NOW, YOU WILL BE MORE DISAPPOINTED BY THE THINGS YOU DIDN'T DO THAN BY THE ONES YOU DID DO, SO **THROW OFF THE BOWLINES**, **SAIL AWAY** FROM THE SAFE HARBOR, CATCH THE TRADE WINDS **IN YOUR SAILS**. **EXPLORE. DREAM. DISCOVER.**

Mark Twain
Writer

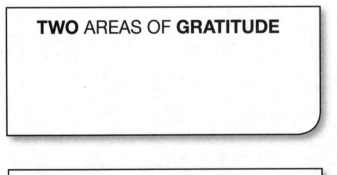

TWO AREAS OF **GRATITUDE**

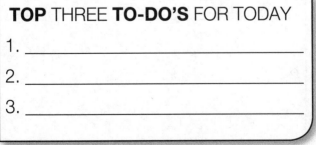

TOP THREE **TO-DO'S** FOR TODAY

1. _____

2. _____

3. _____

THE **BEST** TIME TO **PLANT A TREE** WAS **TWENTY** YEARS AGO. THE **SECOND** BEST TIME **IS NOW.**

Chinese Proverb

TWO AREAS OF **GRATITUDE**

TOP THREE **TO-DO'S** FOR TODAY

1. _____
2. _____
3. _____

YOUR TIME IS **LIMITED**, SO **DON'T WASTE** IT LIVING **SOMEONE** ELSE'S **LIFE**.

Steve Jobs
Cofounder, Chairman, and CEO, Apple Inc.

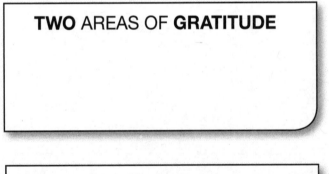

TWO AREAS OF **GRATITUDE**

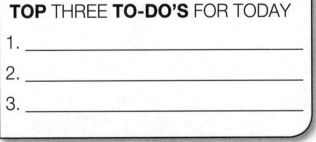

TOP THREE **TO-DO'S** FOR TODAY

1. _____

2. _____

3. _____

YOU CAN **NEVER CROSS THE OCEAN** UNTIL YOU HAVE THE COURAGE TO **LOSE SIGHT** OF THE SHORE.

Christopher Columbus
Italian Explorer, Navigator, and Colonizer

TWO AREAS OF **GRATITUDE**

TOP THREE **TO-DO'S** FOR TODAY

1. _____

2. _____

3. _____

THE TWO MOST IMPORTANT **DAYS OF YOUR LIFE** ARE THE DAY YOU WERE **BORN** AND THE DAY YOU FIND OUT WHY.

Mark Twain
Writer

TWO AREAS OF **GRATITUDE**

TOP THREE **TO-DO'S** FOR TODAY

1. _____

2. _____

3. _____

WHATEVER YOU **CAN DO**, OR **DREAM** YOU CAN, **BEGIN IT. BOLDNESS** HAS **GENIUS, POWER**, AND **MAGIC** IN IT.

Johan Wolfgang von Goethe
German Writer and Statesman

TWO AREAS OF **GRATITUDE**

TOP THREE **TO-DO'S** FOR TODAY

1. _____

2. _____

3. _____

NOTES

PEOPLE OFTEN SAY THAT MOTIVATION DOESN'T LAST. WELL, NEITHER DOES **BATHING**. THAT'S WHY WE RECOMMEND IT **DAILY**.

Zig Ziglar
Motivational Speaker

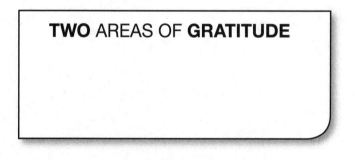

TWO AREAS OF **GRATITUDE**

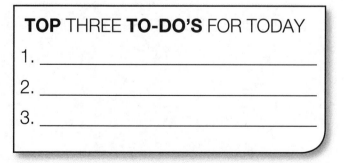

TOP THREE **TO-DO'S** FOR TODAY

1. _____

2. _____

3. _____

THE **ONLY PERSON** YOU ARE **DESTINED** TO BECOME IS THE PERSON YOU **DECIDE TO BE.**

Ralph Waldo Emerson
Essayist, Lecturer, and Poet

TWO AREAS OF **GRATITUDE**

TOP THREE **TO-DO'S** FOR TODAY

1. _____

2. _____

3. _____

GO CONFIDENTLY IN THE DIRECTION **OF YOUR DREAMS.** LIVE THE LIFE YOU HAVE **IMAGINED**.

Henry David Thoreau
Essayist, Poet, and Philosopher

TWO AREAS OF **GRATITUDE**

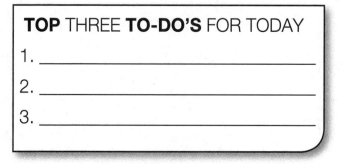

TOP THREE **TO-DO'S** FOR TODAY

1. _____

2. _____

3. _____

WHEN I STAND BEFORE **GOD** AT THE **END OF MY LIFE**, I WOULD HOPE THAT I WOULD **NOT** HAVE A **SINGLE BIT** OF **TALENT LEFT** AND COULD SAY, I USED EVERYTHING YOU GAVE ME.

Erma Bombeck
Humorist, Columnist, and Author

TWO AREAS OF **GRATITUDE**

TOP THREE **TO-DO'S** FOR TODAY

1. _____

2. _____

3. _____

FEW THINGS CAN **HELP** AN INDIVIDUAL MORE THAN TO PLACE **RESPONSIBILITY** ON HIM AND TO LET HIM KNOW YOU TRUST HIM.

Booker T. Washington
Educator, Orator, and Advisor to US Presidents

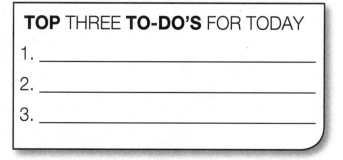

TWO AREAS OF **GRATITUDE**

TOP THREE **TO-DO'S** FOR TODAY

1. _____

2. _____

3. _____

LIFE IS NOT MEASURED BY THE NUMBER OF **BREATHS WE TAKE** BUT BY THE **MOMENTS** THAT TAKE OUR BREATH AWAY.

Maya Angelou
Poet, Memoirist, and Civil Rights Activist

TWO AREAS OF **GRATITUDE**

TOP THREE **TO-DO'S** FOR TODAY

1. _____

2. _____

3. _____

YOU CAN'T **FALL** IF YOU **DON'T CLIMB**. BUT THERE'S **NO JOY** IN LIVING YOUR WHOLE LIFE **ON THE GROUND**.

Unknown

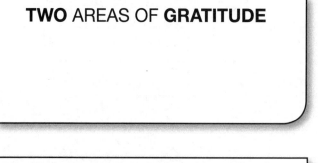

TWO AREAS OF **GRATITUDE**

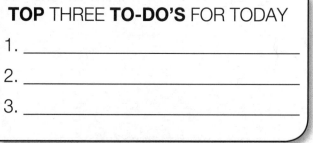

TOP THREE **TO-DO'S** FOR TODAY

1. _____

2. _____

3. _____

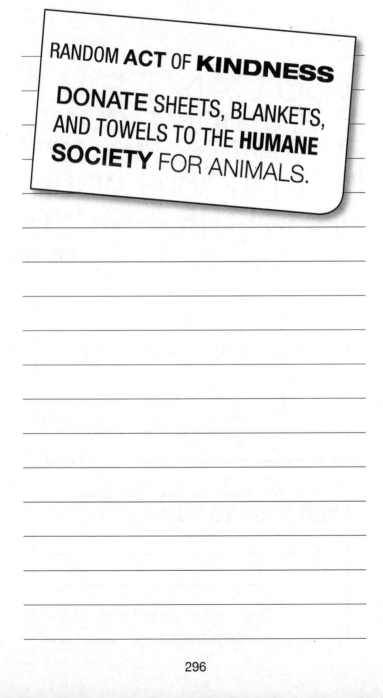

RANDOM **ACT** OF **KINDNESS**

DONATE SHEETS, BLANKETS, AND TOWELS TO THE **HUMANE SOCIETY** FOR ANIMALS.

TOO MANY OF US ARE NOT LIVING OUR DREAMS BECAUSE WE ARE LIVING OUR FEARS.

Les Brown
Motivational Speaker, Radio DJ,
and Former Politician

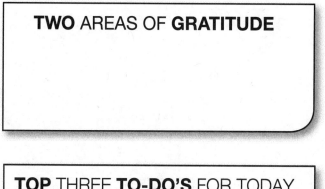

TWO AREAS OF **GRATITUDE**

TOP THREE **TO-DO'S** FOR TODAY

1. _____

2. _____

3. _____

IF YOU WANT TO
LIFT YOURSELF UP,
LIFT UP **SOMEONE ELSE**.

Booker T. Washington
Educator, Orator, and Advisor to US Presidents

TWO AREAS OF **GRATITUDE**

TOP THREE **TO-DO'S** FOR TODAY

1. _____

2. _____

3. _____

LIMITATIONS
LIVE ONLY IN OUR MINDS. BUT IF WE USE OUR
IMAGINATIONS,
OUR POSSIBILITIES BECOME **LIMITLESS**.

Jamie Paolinetti
Actor

TWO AREAS OF **GRATITUDE**

TOP THREE **TO-DO'S** FOR TODAY

1. _____

2. _____

3. _____

YOU TAKE YOUR **LIFE** IN YOUR **OWN HANDS,** AND **WHAT HAPPENS?** A TERRIBLE THING, **NO ONE TO BLAME.**

Erica Jong
Novelist and Poet

TWO AREAS OF **GRATITUDE**

TOP THREE **TO-DO'S** FOR TODAY

1. _____

2. _____

3. _____

I DIDN'T **FAIL** THE TEST. I JUST FOUND **100 WAYS** TO DO IT **WRONG**.

Benjamin Franklin
Author, Printer, and Political Theorist

TWO AREAS OF **GRATITUDE**

TOP THREE **TO-DO'S** FOR TODAY

1. _____
2. _____
3. _____

A PERSON WHO NEVER
MADE A MISTAKE
NEVER TRIED ANYTHING **NEW**.

Albert Einstein
Theoretical Physicist

TWO AREAS OF **GRATITUDE**

TOP THREE **TO-DO'S** FOR TODAY

1. _____

2. _____

3. _____

THE PERSON WHO SAYS **IT CANNOT BE DONE** SHOULD NOT **INTERRUPT** THE PERSON WHO **IS DOING IT.**

Chinese Proverb

TWO AREAS OF **GRATITUDE**

TOP THREE **TO-DO'S** FOR TODAY

1. _____

2. _____

3. _____

NOTES

THERE ARE **NO TRAFFIC JAMS** ALONG THE **EXTRA MILE**.

Roger Staubach
Former Football Quarterback in the NFL

TWO AREAS OF **GRATITUDE**

TOP THREE **TO-DO'S** FOR TODAY

1. _____
2. _____
3. _____

IF YOU WANT YOUR **CHILDREN** TO TURN OUT WELL, SPEND **TWICE** AS MUCH **TIME** WITH THEM AND **HALF AS MUCH MONEY.**

Abigail Van Buren
"Dear Abby" Advice Columnist and
Radio Show Host

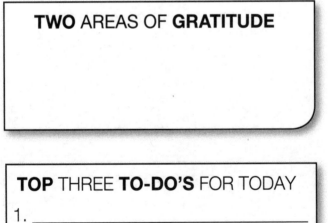

TWO AREAS OF **GRATITUDE**

TOP THREE **TO-DO'S** FOR TODAY

1. _____

2. _____

3. _____

IF YOU LOOK AT WHAT YOU **HAVE** IN LIFE, YOU'LL ALWAYS HAVE MORE. IF YOU LOOK AT WHAT YOU **DON'T HAVE** IN LIFE, YOU'LL NEVER HAVE ENOUGH.

Oprah Winfrey
Media Proprietor

TWO AREAS OF **GRATITUDE**

TOP THREE **TO-DO'S** FOR TODAY

1. _____

2. _____

3. _____

DREAM BIG,
AND **DARE TO FAIL.**

Norman Vaughan
Dogsled Driver and Explorer

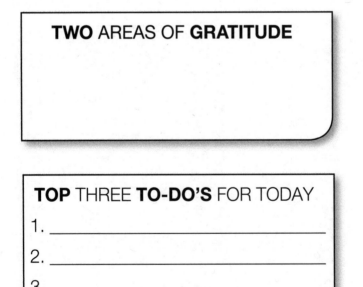

TWO AREAS OF **GRATITUDE**

TOP THREE **TO-DO'S** FOR TODAY

1. _____
2. _____
3. _____

DO **WHAT** YOU **CAN**, **WHERE** YOU **ARE**, WITH **WHAT** YOU **HAVE**.

Theodore Roosevelt
26th US President

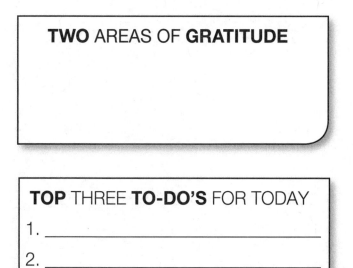

TWO AREAS OF **GRATITUDE**

TOP THREE **TO-DO'S** FOR TODAY

1. _____
2. _____
3. _____

DREAMING, AFTER ALL, IS A FORM OF PLANNING.

Gloria Steinem
Feminist, Journalist, and Social
and Political Activist

TWO AREAS OF **GRATITUDE**

TOP THREE **TO-DO'S** FOR TODAY

1. _____

2. _____

3. _____

IT'S YOUR **PLACE** IN THE **WORLD**;
IT'S YOUR **LIFE**.
GO ON AND DO ALL YOU CAN
WITH IT, AND MAKE IT THE
LIFE YOU WANT TO LIVE.

Mae Jemison
Engineer, Physician, and NASA Astronaut

TWO AREAS OF **GRATITUDE**

TOP THREE **TO-DO'S** FOR TODAY

1. _____

2. _____

3. _____

RANDOM **ACT** OF **KINDNESS**

PAY FOR THE PERSON **BEHIND** YOU AT THE **DRIVE-THRU.**

YOU MAY BE
DISAPPOINTED
IF YOU **FAIL**, BUT YOU ARE
DOOMED IF YOU DON'T TRY.

Beverly Sills
Operatic Soprano

TWO AREAS OF **GRATITUDE**

TOP THREE **TO-DO'S** FOR TODAY

1. _____

2. _____

3. _____

REMEMBER, **NO ONE** CAN MAKE YOU FEEL **INFERIOR WITHOUT YOUR CONSENT.**

Eleanor Roosevelt
Longest-Serving First Lady of the United States

TWO AREAS OF **GRATITUDE**

TOP THREE **TO-DO'S** FOR TODAY

1. _____

2. _____

3. _____

THE **QUESTION** ISN'T
WHO IS GOING TO **LET** ME;
IT'S WHO IS GOING TO **STOP** ME.

Ayn Rand
Russian-American Writer and Philosopher

TWO AREAS OF **GRATITUDE**

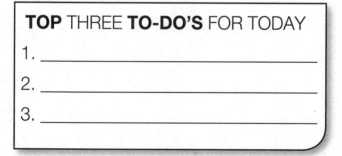

TOP THREE **TO-DO'S** FOR TODAY

1. _____

2. _____

3. _____

IT'S NOT THE YEARS
IN YOUR LIFE THAT COUNT.
IT'S THE LIFE
IN YOUR YEARS.

Abraham Lincoln
16th US President

TWO AREAS OF **GRATITUDE**

TOP THREE **TO-DO'S** FOR TODAY

1. _____

2. _____

3. _____

IF YOUR **ACTIONS** INSPIRE OTHERS TO **DREAM** MORE, **LEARN** MORE, **DO** MORE, AND **BECOME** MORE... YOU ARE A **LEADER**.

John Quincy Adams
6th US President

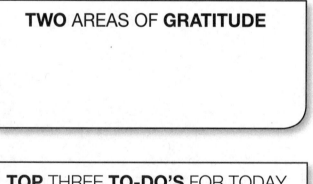

TWO AREAS OF **GRATITUDE**

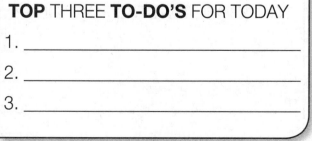

TOP THREE **TO-DO'S** FOR TODAY

1. _____
2. _____
3. _____

THINGS TURN OUT BEST
FOR PEOPLE WHO
MAKE THE BEST
OF THE WAY THINGS TURN OUT.

Art Linkletter
Radio and TV Personality

TWO AREAS OF **GRATITUDE**

TOP THREE **TO-DO'S** FOR TODAY

1. _____

2. _____

3. _____

NOTHING **GREAT** HAS EVER BEEN **ACHIEVED** EXCEPT BY THOSE WHO **DARED** BELIEVE SOMETHING INSIDE THEM WAS **SUPERIOR** TO CIRCUMSTANCE.

Bruce Barton
Author, Advertising Executive, and Politician

TWO AREAS OF **GRATITUDE**

TOP THREE **TO-DO'S** FOR TODAY

1. _____

2. _____

3. _____

NOTES

UNDERSTAND THE **POWER OF GRATITUDE,** AND YOU'LL HAVE A **TRANSFORMATIVE** TOOL FOR LIFE.

Dan Sullivan
Lawyer and Junior US Senator from Alaska

TWO AREAS OF **GRATITUDE**

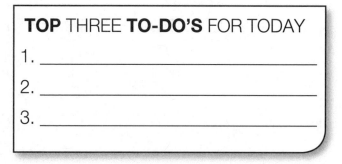

TOP THREE **TO-DO'S** FOR TODAY

1. _____
2. _____
3. _____

THINGS IN LIFE HAPPEN **FOR US, NOT TO US**.

Tony Robbins
Motivational Speaker and Change Catalyst

TWO AREAS OF **GRATITUDE**

TOP THREE **TO-DO'S** FOR TODAY

1. _____
2. _____
3. _____

SUCCESS WITHOUT
FULFILLMENT
IS THE **ULTIMATE FAILURE**.

Tony Robbins
Motivational Speaker and Change Catalyst

TWO AREAS OF **GRATITUDE**

TOP THREE **TO-DO'S** FOR TODAY

1. _____
2. _____
3. _____

YOU HAVE TO BE ABLE **TO RISK YOUR IDENTITY** FOR A BIGGER **FUTURE** THAN THE **PRESENT** YOU ARE LIVING.

Fernando Flores
Chilean Engineer, Entrepreneur, and Politician

TWO AREAS OF **GRATITUDE**

TOP THREE **TO-DO'S** FOR TODAY

1. _____

2. _____

3. _____

PEOPLE BECOME REALLY QUITE **REMARKABLE** WHEN THEY START THINKING THAT THEY **CAN DO THINGS**. WHEN THEY **BELIEVE IN THEMSELVES,** THEY HAVE THE FIRST **SECRET OF SUCCESS.**

Norman Vincent Peale
Minister and Author on Positive Thinking

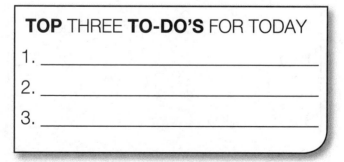

TWO AREAS OF **GRATITUDE**

TOP THREE **TO-DO'S** FOR TODAY

1. _____

2. _____

3. _____

THE PURSUIT OF **PERFECTION** OFTEN IMPEDES **IMPROVEMENT.**

George F. Will
Conservative Political Commentator

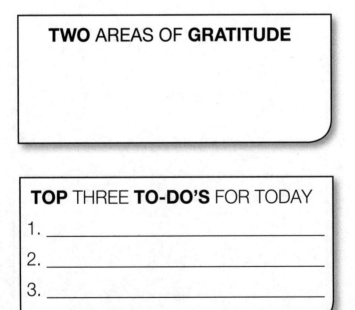

TWO AREAS OF **GRATITUDE**

TOP THREE **TO-DO'S** FOR TODAY

1. _____

2. _____

3. _____

DAY 287: DATE: _____

WHEN I LOOK BACK ON ALL (MY) WORRIES, I REMEMBER THE STORY OF THE **OLD MAN** WHO SAID ON HIS DEATHBED **THAT HE HAD HAD A LOT OF TROUBLE IN HIS LIFE,** MOST OF WHICH HAD **NEVER HAPPENED**.

Winston Churchill
Former Prime Minister of the United Kingdom

TWO AREAS OF **GRATITUDE**

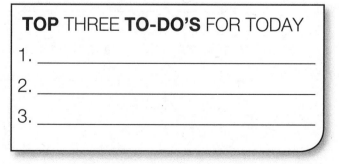

TOP THREE **TO-DO'S** FOR TODAY

1. _____

2. _____

3. _____

RANDOM **ACT** OF **KINDNESS**

DONATE BOOKS TO THE LIBRARY.

MAY YOUR **TROUBLES BE LESS** AND YOUR **BLESSINGS BE MORE** AND NOTHING BUT **HAPPINESS** COME THROUGH YOUR DOOR.

Irish Blessing

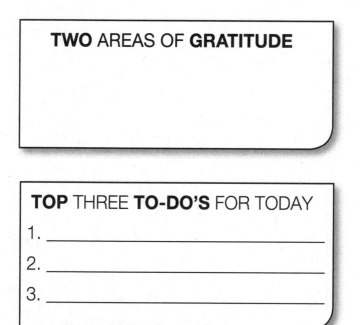

TWO AREAS OF **GRATITUDE**

TOP THREE **TO-DO'S** FOR TODAY

1. _____
2. _____
3. _____

EXPERIENCES YOU RECALL ARE RECOLLECTIONS. EXPERIENCES YOU FEEL **ARE MEMORIES.**

Lee Brower
Author on Wealth Preservation

TWO AREAS OF **GRATITUDE**

TOP THREE **TO-DO'S** FOR TODAY

1. _____

2. _____

3. _____

MOST PEOPLE NEVER RUN FAR ENOUGH ON THEIR **FIRST WIND** TO FIND OUT IF THEY'VE GOT A **SECOND. GIVE YOUR DREAMS ALL YOU'VE GOT,** AND YOU'LL BE AMAZED AT THE **ENERGY THAT COMES OUT OF YOU.**

William Jones
Author

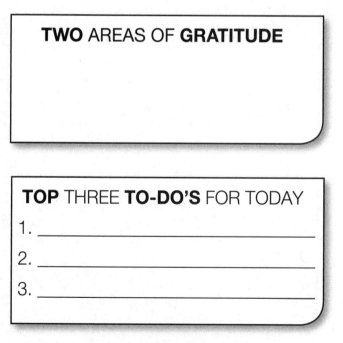

TWO AREAS OF **GRATITUDE**

TOP THREE **TO-DO'S** FOR TODAY

1. _____
2. _____
3. _____

DON'T BE AFRAID TO **GIVE UP THE GOOD** TO GO FOR THE **GREAT.**

John D. Rockefeller

Oil Industry Business Magnate and Philanthropist

TWO AREAS OF **GRATITUDE**

TOP THREE **TO-DO'S** FOR TODAY

1. _____

2. _____

3. _____

LIFE IS LIKE A CAMERA.
FOCUS ON WHAT'S IMPORTANT,
CAPTURE THE GOOD TIMES,
DEVELOP FROM THE NEGATIVES,
AND IF THINGS DON'T WORK OUT,
TAKE ANOTHER SHOT.

Ziad K. Abdelnour
Author

TWO AREAS OF **GRATITUDE**

TOP THREE **TO-DO'S** FOR TODAY

1. _____
2. _____
3. _____

KID, YOU'LL MOVE
MOUNTAINS!

Dr. Seuss
Political Cartoonist, Poet, Animator,
and Children's Book Author

TWO AREAS OF **GRATITUDE**

TOP THREE **TO-DO'S** FOR TODAY

1. _____

2. _____

3. _____

WHAT YOU **GET**
BY ACHIEVING YOUR GOALS
IS NOT AS IMPORTANT AS
WHAT YOU **BECOME**
BY ACHIEVING YOUR GOALS.

Zig Ziglar
Motivational Speaker

TWO AREAS OF **GRATITUDE**

TOP THREE **TO-DO'S** FOR TODAY

1. _____

2. _____

3. _____

NOTES

YOUR **ATTITUDE**, NOT YOUR APTITUDE, WILL DETERMINE YOUR **ALTITUDE.**

Zig Ziglar
Motivational Speaker

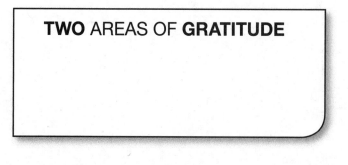

TWO AREAS OF **GRATITUDE**

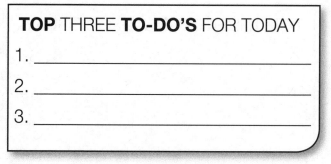

TOP THREE **TO-DO'S** FOR TODAY

1. _____
2. _____
3. _____

LEARN TO ENJOY EVERY MINUTE OF YOUR LIFE.
BE HAPPY NOW.
DON'T WAIT FOR SOMETHING OUTSIDE OF YOURSELF TO MAKE YOU HAPPY IN THE FUTURE.
THINK HOW REALLY PRECIOUS IS THE TIME YOU HAVE TO SPEND,
WHETHER IT'S AT WORK OR WITH YOUR FAMILY.
EVERY MINUTE SHOULD BE ENJOYED AND SAVORED.

Earl Nightingale
Radio Personality and Author on Human
Character Development

TWO AREAS OF **GRATITUDE**

TOP THREE **TO-DO'S** FOR TODAY

1. _____
2. _____
3. _____

A **HUG** IS A
PERFECT GIFT.
ONE SIZE FITS ALL, AND NOBODY MINDS
IF YOU EXCHANGE IT.

Unknown

TWO AREAS OF **GRATITUDE**

TOP THREE **TO-DO'S** FOR TODAY

1. _____

2. _____

3. _____

IT IS A VERY **FUNNY THING ABOUT LIFE**: IF YOU REFUSE TO ACCEPT **ANYTHING BUT THE BEST**, YOU VERY OFTEN **GET IT**.

W. Somerset Maugham
British Playwright and Writer

TWO AREAS OF **GRATITUDE**

TOP THREE **TO-DO'S** FOR TODAY

1. _____

2. _____

3. _____

YOU CAN HAVE
MORE THAN YOU'VE GOT
BECAUSE YOU CAN BECOME
MORE THAN YOU ARE.

Jim Rohn
Motivational Speaker and Author

TWO AREAS OF **GRATITUDE**

TOP THREE **TO-DO'S** FOR TODAY

1. _____

2. _____

3. _____

A **HAPPY** LIFE
CONSISTS **NOT** IN THE **ABSENCE**
BUT THE **MASTERY**
OF **HARDSHIPS**.

Helen Keller
Writer and Political Activist

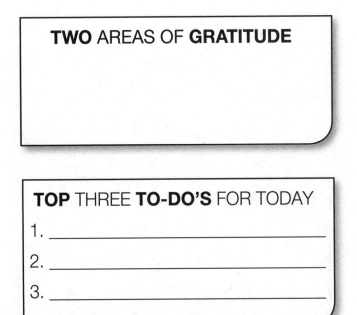

TWO AREAS OF **GRATITUDE**

TOP THREE **TO-DO'S** FOR TODAY

1. _____

2. _____

3. _____

MOST OF THE **IMPORTANT THINGS** IN THE WORLD HAVE BEEN **ACCOMPLISHED** BY PEOPLE WHO HAVE **KEPT ON TRYING** WHEN THERE SEEMED TO BE **NO HOPE AT ALL**.

Dale Carnegie
Writer, Lecturer, and Developer of
Self-Improvement Courses

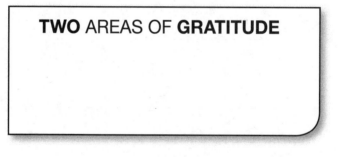

TWO AREAS OF **GRATITUDE**

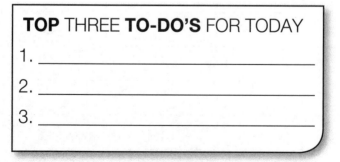

TOP THREE **TO-DO'S** FOR TODAY

1. _____
2. _____
3. _____

RANDOM **ACT** OF **KINDNESS**

GIVE SOMEONE
A HUG.

DAY 302: DATE: _____

YOU HAVE NOT LIVED **A PERFECT DAY** UNLESS YOU HAVE DONE **SOMETHING FOR SOMEONE** WHO WILL **NEVER** BE ABLE TO **REPAY** YOU.

Ruth Smeltzer
Author

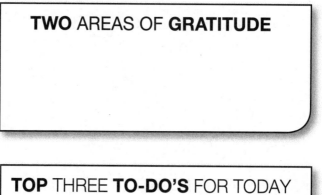

TWO AREAS OF **GRATITUDE**

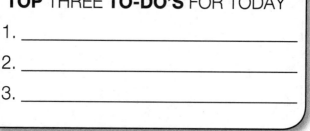

TOP THREE **TO-DO'S** FOR TODAY

1. _____

2. _____

3. _____

WHEN YOU **FACE YOUR FEAR**, MOST OF THE TIME YOU WILL DISCOVER THAT IT WAS **NOT REALLY** SUCH A **BIG THREAT** AFTER ALL. **WE ALL NEED** SOME FORM OF DEEPLY ROOTED, **POWERFUL MOTIVATION** — IT EMPOWERS US TO **OVERCOME OBSTACLES** SO WE CAN **LIVE OUR DREAMS**.

Les Brown
Motivational Speaker, Radio DJ,
and Former Politician

TWO AREAS OF **GRATITUDE**

TOP THREE **TO-DO'S** FOR TODAY

1. _____

2. _____

3. _____

THE MOST IMPORTANT THING IN **LIFE** IS TO **STOP SAYING 'I WISH'** AND **START SAYING 'I WILL.'** CONSIDER **NOTHING IMPOSSIBLE**, THEN TREAT POSSIBILITIES AS **PROBABILITIES**.

Charles Dickens
English Writer and Social Critic

TWO AREAS OF **GRATITUDE**

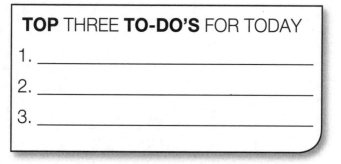

TOP THREE **TO-DO'S** FOR TODAY

1. _____

2. _____

3. _____

YOU CAN'T
CHANGE THE PAST,
BUT YOU CAN **RUIN**
A PERFECTLY GOOD **PRESENT**
BY **WORRYING** ABOUT
THE FUTURE.

Isak Dinesen
Danish Author

TWO AREAS OF **GRATITUDE**

TOP THREE **TO-DO'S** FOR TODAY

1. _____

2. _____

3. _____

SO MANY OF OUR DREAMS
AT FIRST SEEM **IMPOSSIBLE**,
THEN THEY SEEM **IMPROBABLE**,
AND THEN, WHEN WE
SUMMON THE WILL,
THEY SOON BECOME
INEVITABLE.

Christopher Reeve
Actor, Film Director, Producer, and Activist

TWO AREAS OF **GRATITUDE**

TOP THREE **TO-DO'S** FOR TODAY

1. _____

2. _____

3. _____

EACH TIME YOU ARE **HONEST** AND CONDUCT YOURSELF WITH **HONESTY**, A **SUCCESS FORCE** WILL DRIVE YOU TOWARD **GREATER SUCCESS**. EACH TIME YOU **LIE**, EVEN WITH A LITTLE WHITE LIE, THERE ARE **STRONG FORCES** PUSHING YOU TOWARD **FAILURE**.

Joseph Sugarman
Author and Copywriting Specialist

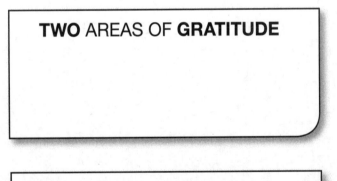

TWO AREAS OF **GRATITUDE**

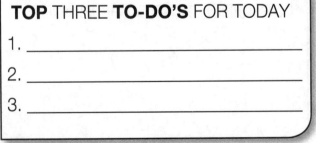

TOP THREE **TO-DO'S** FOR TODAY

1. _____

2. _____

3. _____

THE **BIGGEST** HUMAN TEMPTATION IS TO **SETTLE** FOR **TOO LITTLE**.

Thomas Merton
Catholic Writer, Theologian, Mystic,
and Trappist Monk

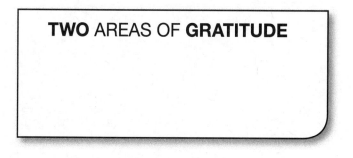

TWO AREAS OF **GRATITUDE**

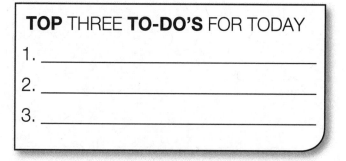

TOP THREE **TO-DO'S** FOR TODAY

1. _____

2. _____

3. _____

NOTES

LIFE IS NOT A **JOURNEY TO THE GRAVE** WITH THE INTENTION OF **ARRIVING SAFELY** IN A PRETTY AND WELL-PRESERVED BODY, BUT RATHER **THE PLAN IS TO SKID IN BROADSIDE,** THOROUGHLY USED UP, TOTALLY WORN OUT, AND LOUDLY PROCLAIMING, **'WOW — WHAT A RIDE!'**

Unknown

TWO AREAS OF **GRATITUDE**

TOP THREE **TO-DO'S** FOR TODAY

1. _____

2. _____

3. _____

THE **MORE YOU PRAISE** AND **CELEBRATE** YOUR **LIFE,** THE **MORE THERE IS IN LIFE** TO CELEBRATE.

Oprah Winfrey
Media Proprietor

TWO AREAS OF **GRATITUDE**

TOP THREE **TO-DO'S** FOR TODAY

1. _____

2. _____

3. _____

HAPPINESS CANNOT BE TRAVELED TO, OWNED, EARNED, OR WORN. IT IS THE SPIRITUAL EXPERIENCE OF LIVING EVERY MINUTE WITH LOVE, GRACE, AND GRATITUDE.

Denis Waitley
Motivational Speaker, Writer, and
Consultant on Winning

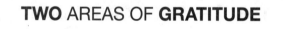

TWO AREAS OF **GRATITUDE**

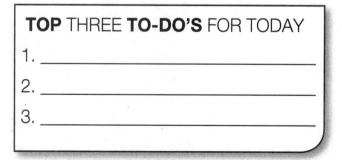

TOP THREE **TO-DO'S** FOR TODAY

1. _____

2. _____

3. _____

THE **TRUTH** OF THE MATTER IS THAT **YOU ALWAYS KNOW** THE **RIGHT THING** TO DO. THE HARD PART IS **DOING IT**.

Norman Schwarzkopf, Jr.
US Army General, Gulf War

TWO AREAS OF **GRATITUDE**

TOP THREE **TO-DO'S** FOR TODAY

1. _____

2. _____

3. _____

PATIENCE AND PERSEVERANCE HAVE A **MAGICAL EFFECT** BEFORE WHICH **DIFFICULTIES DISAPPEAR** AND OBSTACLES VANISH. A **LITTLE** KNOWLEDGE **THAT ACTS** IS WORTH **INFINITELY MORE** THAN **MUCH KNOWLEDGE** THAT IS **IDLE**.

John Quincy Adams
6th US President

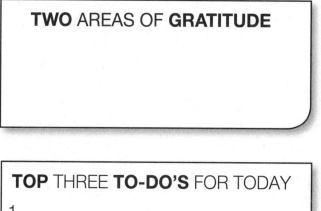

TWO AREAS OF **GRATITUDE**

TOP THREE **TO-DO'S** FOR TODAY

1. _____

2. _____

3. _____

IF YOU PUT OFF EVERYTHING TILL YOU'RE SURE OF IT, YOU'LL **NEVER** GET **ANYTHING DONE**.

Norman Vincent Peale
Minister and Author on Positive Thinking

TWO AREAS OF **GRATITUDE**

TOP THREE **TO-DO'S** FOR TODAY

1. _____
2. _____
3. _____

PROFOUND COMMITMENT TO A **DREAM** DOES NOT **CONFINE** OR **CONSTRAIN**; IT LIBERATES. EVEN A DIFFICULT, WINDING PATH CAN **LEAD TO YOUR GOAL** IF YOU **FOLLOW IT TO THE END**.

Paulo Coelho
Brazilian Author

TWO AREAS OF **GRATITUDE**

TOP THREE **TO-DO'S** FOR TODAY

1. _____

2. _____

3. _____

RANDOM **ACT** OF **KINDNESS**

TAKE **TREATS** TO A
FIRE/POLICE STATION
WITH A **THANK YOU** NOTE.

WHEN YOU **CAN'T CONTROL** WHAT'S HAPPENING, CHALLENGE YOURSELF **TO CONTROL THE** WAY YOU RESPOND TO WHAT'S HAPPENING. THAT'S WHERE YOUR **POWER** IS!

Unknown

TWO AREAS OF **GRATITUDE**

TOP THREE **TO-DO'S** FOR TODAY

1. _____
2. _____
3. _____

THE BIGGEST
COMMUNICATION PROBLEM
IS WE **DO NOT LISTEN**
TO **UNDERSTAND**;
WE LISTEN TO **REPLY**.

Stephen Covey
Educator, Author, and Keynote Speaker

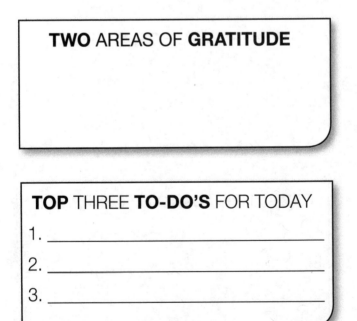

TWO AREAS OF **GRATITUDE**

TOP THREE **TO-DO'S** FOR TODAY

1. _____

2. _____

3. _____

DAY 318: DATE: _____

YOU HAVE A **CLEAN SLATE EVERY DAY** YOU WAKE UP. YOU HAVE A CHANCE **EVERY** SINGLE MORNING TO **MAKE THAT CHANGE** AND **BE** THE PERSON YOU WANT TO BE. YOU JUST HAVE TO **DECIDE TO DO IT**. **DECIDE TODAY'S THE DAY.** SAY IT: THIS IS GOING TO BE **MY DAY**.

Brendon Burchard
Author on Motivation and the Use of
Digital and Affiliate Marketing

TWO AREAS OF **GRATITUDE**

TOP THREE **TO-DO'S** FOR TODAY

1. _____

2. _____

3. _____

RECOGNIZING THAT YOU ARE **NOT** WHERE YOU **WANT TO BE** IS A STARTING POINT TO BEGIN **CHANGING YOUR LIFE**.

Deborah Day
Licensed Mental Health Counselor

TWO AREAS OF **GRATITUDE**

TOP THREE **TO-DO'S** FOR TODAY

1. _____
2. _____
3. _____

POSITIVE THINKING IS MORE THAN **JUST A TAGLINE.** IT **CHANGES** THE WAY WE **BEHAVE**. AND I **FIRMLY BELIEVE** THAT WHEN I AM **POSITIVE**, IT NOT ONLY MAKES **ME BETTER**, BUT IT ALSO MAKES **THOSE AROUND ME BETTER**.

Harvey Mackay
Businessman and Author

TWO AREAS OF **GRATITUDE**

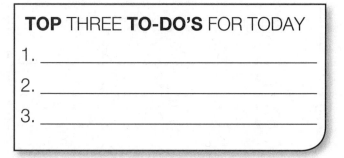

TOP THREE **TO-DO'S** FOR TODAY

1. _____
2. _____
3. _____

OUR **DEEPEST FEAR** IS **NOT** THAT **WE ARE INADEQUATE**. OUR DEEPEST FEAR IS THAT WE ARE **POWERFUL BEYOND MEASURE**. IT IS **OUR LIGHT**, NOT OUR DARKNESS, THAT MOST **FRIGHTENS US**. WE ASK OURSELVES, WHO AM I TO BE **BRILLIANT**, **GORGEOUS**, **TALENTED**, AND **FABULOUS**? ACTUALLY, **WHO ARE YOU NOT TO BE?**

Marianne Williamson
Spiritual Teacher, Lecturer, and Author

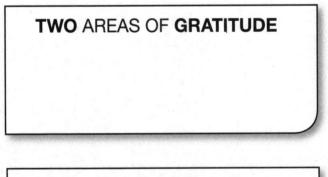

TWO AREAS OF **GRATITUDE**

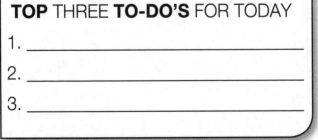

TOP THREE **TO-DO'S** FOR TODAY

1. _____

2. _____

3. _____

YOU ARE ONLY ONE DECISION AWAY FROM A TOTALLY DIFFERENT LIFE.

Unknown

TWO AREAS OF **GRATITUDE**

TOP THREE **TO-DO'S** FOR TODAY

1. _____

2. _____

3. _____

NOTES

EVERY GREAT **DREAM** BEGINS WITH A **DREAMER**. ALWAYS REMEMBER, YOU HAVE **WITHIN YOU** THE **STRENGTH**, THE **PATIENCE**, AND THE **PASSION** TO REACH FOR THE STARS TO **CHANGE THE WORLD**.

Harriet Tubman
Abolitionist and Humanitarian

TWO AREAS OF **GRATITUDE**

TOP THREE **TO-DO'S** FOR TODAY

1. _____

2. _____

3. _____

I FIND IT **FASCINATING** THAT MOST PEOPLE **PLAN THEIR VACATIONS** WITH **BETTER CARE** THAN THEY DO **THEIR LIVES**. PERHAPS THAT IS BECAUSE **ESCAPE** IS EASIER THAN **CHANGE**.

Jim Rohn
Motivational Speaker and Author

TWO AREAS OF **GRATITUDE**

TOP THREE **TO-DO'S** FOR TODAY

1. _____

2. _____

3. _____

OUR GREATEST WEAKNESS LIES IN **GIVING UP**... THE MOST CERTAIN WAY **TO SUCCEED** IS **ALWAYS TO TRY JUST ONE MORE TIME.**

Thomas Edison
Inventor and Businessman

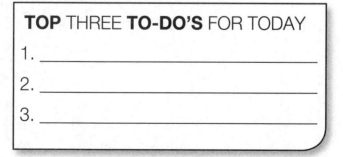

TWO AREAS OF **GRATITUDE**

TOP THREE **TO-DO'S** FOR TODAY

1. _____

2. _____

3. _____

LET TODAY BE THE DAY YOU FINALLY **RELEASE YOURSELF** FROM THE **IMPRISONMENT** OF **PAST GRUDGES AND ANGER**. SIMPLIFY YOUR LIFE. LET GO OF THE **POISONOUS PAST**, AND LIVE THE ABUNDANTLY BEAUTIFUL PRESENT...**TODAY**.

Steve Maraboli
Motivational Speaker

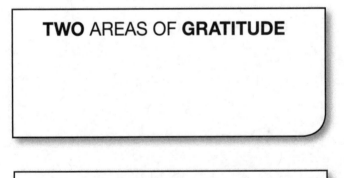

TWO AREAS OF **GRATITUDE**

TOP THREE **TO-DO'S** FOR TODAY

1. _____
2. _____
3. _____

GOOD THINGS COME TO THOSE WHO **BELIEVE**. **BETTER THINGS** COME TO THOSE WHO ARE **PATIENT**, AND THE **BEST THINGS** COME TO THOSE WHO **DON'T GIVE UP.**

Unknown

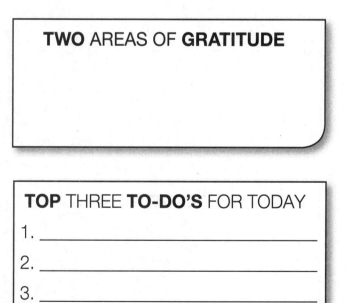

TWO AREAS OF **GRATITUDE**

TOP THREE **TO-DO'S** FOR TODAY

1. _____

2. _____

3. _____

THE CHOICE TO HAVE A **GREAT ATTITUDE** IS SOMETHING THAT **NOBODY** OR **NO CIRCUMSTANCE** CAN TAKE FROM YOU.

Zig Ziglar
Motivational Speaker

TWO AREAS OF **GRATITUDE**

TOP THREE **TO-DO'S** FOR TODAY

1. _____
2. _____
3. _____

FINISH EACH DAY AND BE DONE WITH IT. YOU HAVE DONE WHAT YOU COULD. SOME **BLUNDERS** AND **ABSURDITIES** NO DOUBT CREPT IN; **FORGET THEM** AS SOON AS YOU CAN. TOMORROW IS A NEW DAY. YOU SHALL **BEGIN IT SERENELY** AND WITH **TOO HIGH A SPIRIT** TO BE ENCUMBERED WITH YOUR **OLD NONSENSE**.

Ralph Waldo Emerson
Essayist, Lecturer, and Poet

TWO AREAS OF **GRATITUDE**

TOP THREE **TO-DO'S** FOR TODAY

1. _____

2. _____

3. _____

RANDOM **ACT** OF **KINDNESS**

SHOW OFF YOUR **BEST SMILE** ALL DAY.

NEVER GIVE UP ON A **DREAM** JUST BECAUSE OF THE **TIME** IT WILL TAKE TO **ACCOMPLISH** IT. THE **TIME WILL PASS** ANYWAY.

Earl Nightingale
Radio Personality and Author on Human
Character Development

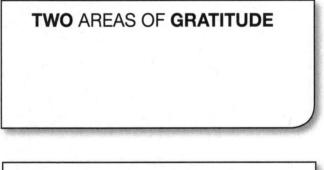

TWO AREAS OF **GRATITUDE**

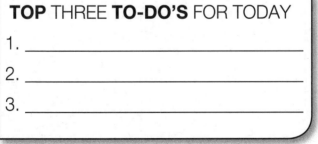

TOP THREE **TO-DO'S** FOR TODAY

1. _____

2. _____

3. _____

SOMETIMES IT IS **BETTER TO BE KIND** THAN TO BE **RIGHT**. WE **DO NOT** NEED AN **INTELLIGENT MIND** THAT **SPEAKS**, BUT A PATIENT HEART THAT LISTENS.

Unknown

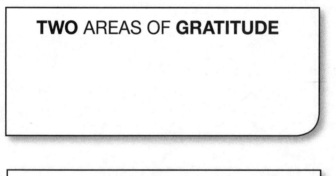

TWO AREAS OF **GRATITUDE**

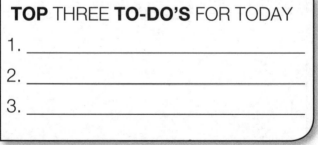

TOP THREE **TO-DO'S** FOR TODAY

1. _____
2. _____
3. _____

GRATITUDE CAN TURN A **NEGATIVE** INTO A **POSITIVE.** FIND A WAY TO BE THANKFUL FOR YOUR **TROUBLES**, AND THEY CAN BECOME **YOUR BLESSINGS.**

Unknown

TWO AREAS OF **GRATITUDE**

TOP THREE **TO-DO'S** FOR TODAY

1. _____

2. _____

3. _____

BELIEFS HAVE THE POWER TO **CREATE** AND THE **POWER TO DESTROY**. **HUMAN BEINGS** HAVE THE AWESOME ABILITY TO **TAKE ANY EXPERIENCE** OF THEIR LIVES AND **CREATE A MEANING** THAT **DISEMPOWERS THEM** OR ONE THAT CAN **LITERALLY SAVE THEIR LIVES**.

Tony Robbins
Motivational Speaker and Change Catalyst

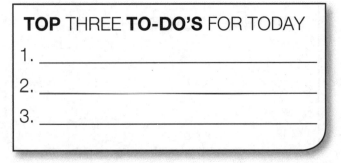

TWO AREAS OF **GRATITUDE**

TOP THREE **TO-DO'S** FOR TODAY

1. _____

2. _____

3. _____

OUT OF **CLUTTER**, FIND **SIMPLICITY**. FROM **DISCORD**, FIND **HARMONY**. IN THE MIDDLE OF **DIFFICULTY** LIES **OPPORTUNITY**.

Albert Einstein
Theoretical Physicist

TWO AREAS OF **GRATITUDE**

TOP THREE **TO-DO'S** FOR TODAY

1. _____

2. _____

3. _____

OPTIMISM IS A HAPPINESS MAGNET.
IF YOU STAY **POSITIVE**, **GOOD THINGS** AND **GOOD PEOPLE** WILL BE **DRAWN TO YOU**.

Mary Lou Retton
Retired Olympic Gymnast

TWO AREAS OF **GRATITUDE**

TOP THREE **TO-DO'S** FOR TODAY

1. _____

2. _____

3. _____

APPRECIATION
IS A WONDERFUL THING;
IT MAKES WHAT IS **EXCELLENT**
IN OTHERS BELONG
TO US AS WELL.

Voltaire
French Enlightenment Writer and Philosopher

TWO AREAS OF **GRATITUDE**

TOP THREE **TO-DO'S** FOR TODAY

1. _____

2. _____

3. _____

NOTES

DAY 337: DATE: _____

GRATITUDE UNLOCKS THE FULLNESS OF **LIFE**. IT TURNS **WHAT WE HAVE INTO ENOUGH, AND MORE.** IT TURNS **DENIAL** INTO **ACCEPTANCE**, **CHAOS** TO **ORDER, CONFUSION** TO **CLARITY.** IT CAN TURN A **MEAL** INTO A **FEAST**, **A HOUSE INTO A HOME, A STRANGER INTO A FRIEND. GRATITUDE** MAKES SENSE OF OUR **PAST**, BRINGS **PEACE FOR TODAY**, AND CREATES A **VISION FOR TOMORROW**.

Melody Beattie
Author

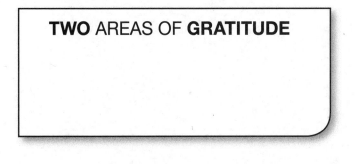

TWO AREAS OF **GRATITUDE**

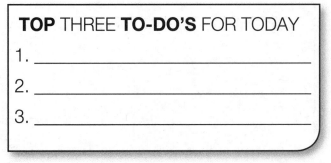

TOP THREE **TO-DO'S** FOR TODAY

1. _____
2. _____
3. _____

OBSTACLES CAN'T STOP YOU.
PROBLEMS CAN'T STOP YOU.
MOST OF ALL, **OTHER PEOPLE**
CAN'T STOP YOU.
ONLY **YOU** CAN STOP YOU.

Unknown

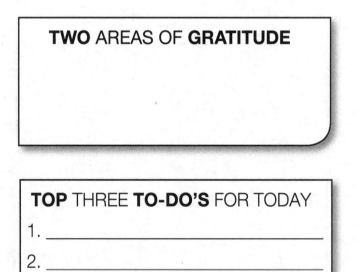

TWO AREAS OF **GRATITUDE**

TOP THREE **TO-DO'S** FOR TODAY

1. _____

2. _____

3. _____

A **HAPPY** PERSON IS **NOT** A PERSON IN A CERTAIN SET OF CIRCUMSTANCES, BUT RATHER A PERSON WITH A CERTAIN SET OF **ATTITUDES**.

Hugh Downs
News Anchor, TV Producer, and Game-Show Host

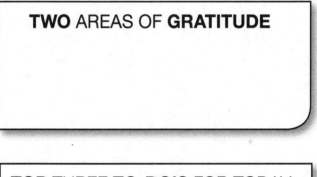

TWO AREAS OF **GRATITUDE**

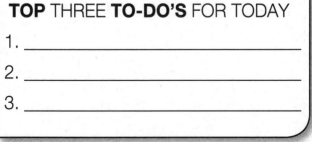

TOP THREE **TO-DO'S** FOR TODAY

1. _____

2. _____

3. _____

LIFE IS NOT SO MUCH A FIGHT TO BE FOUGHT, A GAME TO BE PLAYED, OR A PRIZE TO BE WON. IT'S MORE NEARLY A WORK TO BE DONE AND A LEGACY TO BE LEFT.

William Arthur Ward
Inspirational Writer

TWO AREAS OF **GRATITUDE**

TOP THREE **TO-DO'S** FOR TODAY

1. _____

2. _____

3. _____

I BEGAN LEARNING LONG AGO
THAT THOSE WHO ARE
HAPPIEST
ARE THOSE WHO **DO** THE
MOST FOR OTHERS.

Booker T. Washington
Educator, Orator, and Advisor to US Presidents

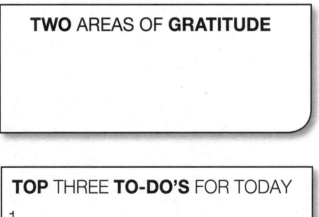

TWO AREAS OF **GRATITUDE**

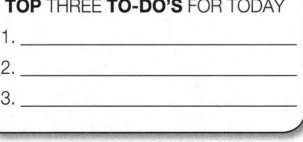

TOP THREE **TO-DO'S** FOR TODAY

1. _____

2. _____

3. _____

THE WORLD NEEDS DREAMERS,
AND THE WORLD NEEDS **DOERS**.
BUT ABOVE ALL, THE WORLD NEEDS DREAMERS WHO DO.

Sarah Ban Breathnach
Author, Philanthropist, and Public Speaker

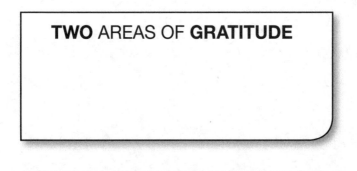

TWO AREAS OF **GRATITUDE**

TOP THREE **TO-DO'S** FOR TODAY

1. _____

2. _____

3. _____

WE ARE ALL HERE **FOR SOME SPECIAL REASON.** STOP BEING A **PRISONER** OF YOUR PAST. BECOME THE **ARCHITECT** OF YOUR FUTURE.

Robin Sharma
Canadian Writer and Leadership Speaker

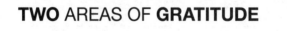

TWO AREAS OF **GRATITUDE**

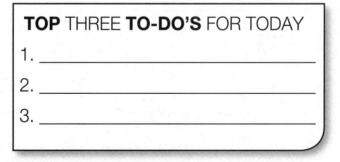

TOP THREE **TO-DO'S** FOR TODAY

1. _____
2. _____
3. _____

RANDOM **ACT** OF **KINDNESS**

PUT YOUR **PHONE AWAY** AND **LISTEN**.

I AM **DETERMINED** TO BE
CHEERFUL AND HAPPY
IN **WHATEVER SITUATION** I MAY
FIND MYSELF. FOR I HAVE LEARNED
THAT THE **GREATER PART** OF OUR
MISERY OR UNHAPPINESS
IS DETERMINED **NOT** BY
OUR **CIRCUMSTANCE**
BUT BY OUR **DISPOSITION**.

Martha Washington
Wife of George Washington, 1st US President

TWO AREAS OF **GRATITUDE**

TOP THREE **TO-DO'S** FOR TODAY

1. _____

2. _____

3. _____

ONE HALF OF **LIFE** IS **LUCK**; THE OTHER HALF IS **DISCIPLINE** — AND THAT'S THE **IMPORTANT** HALF, FOR **WITHOUT DISCIPLINE** YOU WOULDN'T KNOW WHAT TO DO WITH **LUCK**.

Carl Zuckmayer
German Writer and Playwright

TWO AREAS OF **GRATITUDE**

TOP THREE **TO-DO'S** FOR TODAY

1. _____

2. _____

3. _____

WE ARE ALL FACED WITH A SERIES OF **GREAT OPPORTUNITIES** BRILLIANTLY **DISGUISED** AS IMPOSSIBLE SITUATIONS.

Charles R. Swindoll
Pastor, Author, Educator, and Radio Preacher

TWO AREAS OF **GRATITUDE**

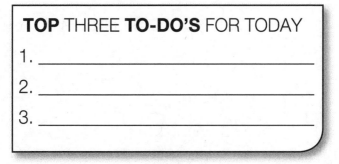

TOP THREE **TO-DO'S** FOR TODAY

1. _____
2. _____
3. _____

AS WE EXPRESS OUR GRATITUDE, WE MUST **NEVER FORGET** THAT THE **HIGHEST APPRECIATION** IS NOT TO **UTTER** WORDS, BUT TO **LIVE** BY THEM.

John F. Kennedy
35th US President

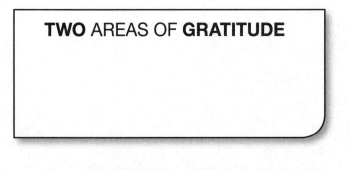

TWO AREAS OF **GRATITUDE**

TOP THREE **TO-DO'S** FOR TODAY

1. _____

2. _____

3. _____

DAY 348: DATE: _____

AS I LOOK BACK ON MY **LIFE**, I REALIZE THAT **EVERY TIME** I **THOUGHT** I WAS BEING **REJECTED** FROM SOMETHING **GOOD**, I WAS ACTUALLY BEING **REDIRECTED** TO SOMETHING **BETTER**.

Steve Maraboli
Motivational Speaker

TWO AREAS OF **GRATITUDE**

TOP THREE **TO-DO'S** FOR TODAY

1. _____

2. _____

3. _____

DREAMS AND DEDICATION ARE A POWERFUL COMBINATION.

William Longgood
Author

TWO AREAS OF **GRATITUDE**

TOP THREE **TO-DO'S** FOR TODAY

1. _____

2. _____

3. _____

IF IT DOESN'T
CHALLENGE YOU,
IT WON'T **CHANGE** YOU.

Fred DeVito
Fitness Trainer

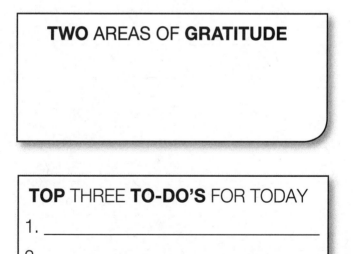

TWO AREAS OF **GRATITUDE**

TOP THREE **TO-DO'S** FOR TODAY

1. _____

2. _____

3. _____

NOTES

BE **SOMEBODY** WHO MAKES **EVERYBODY** FEEL LIKE A **SOMEBODY**.

Robby Novak
American Personality Who Portrays Kid President

TWO AREAS OF **GRATITUDE**

TOP THREE **TO-DO'S** FOR TODAY

1. _____

2. _____

3. _____

DON'T **COUNT** THE **DAYS**; MAKE THE **DAYS COUNT**.

Muhammad Ali
Professional Boxer and Activist

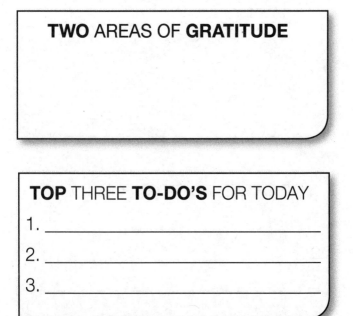

TWO AREAS OF **GRATITUDE**

TOP THREE **TO-DO'S** FOR TODAY

1. _____

2. _____

3. _____

DON'T **WAIT** FOR THE **PERFECT MOMENT**; TAKE THE MOMENT AND **MAKE IT PERFECT**.

Zoe Sayward
Drummer and Reggae Rapper

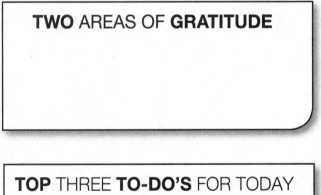

TWO AREAS OF **GRATITUDE**

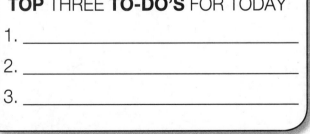

TOP THREE **TO-DO'S** FOR TODAY

1. _____
2. _____
3. _____

WHEN YOU **TALK**, YOU ARE
ONLY REPEATING
WHAT YOU **ALREADY KNOW**.
BUT IF YOU **LISTEN**, YOU MAY
LEARN SOMETHING NEW.

The Dalai Lama

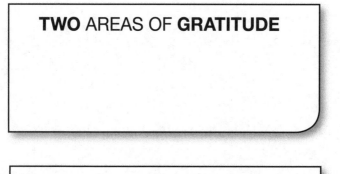

TWO AREAS OF **GRATITUDE**

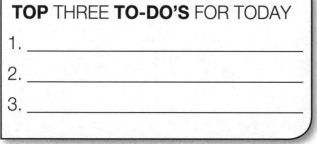

TOP THREE **TO-DO'S** FOR TODAY

1. _____

2. _____

3. _____

I AM **IN CHARGE** OF **HOW I FEEL,** AND **TODAY,** I AM CHOOSING **HAPPINESS**.

Unknown

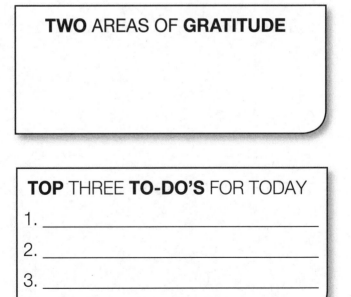

TWO AREAS OF **GRATITUDE**

TOP THREE **TO-DO'S** FOR TODAY

1. _____

2. _____

3. _____

A **DREAM** DOESN'T BECOME **REALITY THROUGH MAGIC;** IT TAKES **SWEAT**, DETERMINATION, AND **HARD WORK**.

Colin Powell
Retired Four-Star General, US Army

TWO AREAS OF **GRATITUDE**

TOP THREE **TO-DO'S** FOR TODAY

1. _____

2. _____

3. _____

ALWAYS **REMEMBER** YOU HAVE WITHIN YOU THE **STRENGTH**, THE **PATIENCE**, AND THE **PASSION** TO REACH FOR THE STARS TO **CHANGE THE WORLD.**

Harriet Tubman
Abolitionist and Humanitarian

TWO AREAS OF **GRATITUDE**

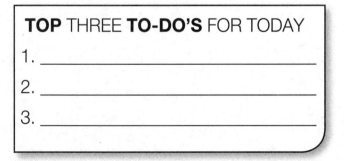

TOP THREE **TO-DO'S** FOR TODAY

1. _____

2. _____

3. _____

RANDOM **ACT** OF **KINDNESS**

LEAVE A **GREAT BIG TIP** FOR YOUR SERVER!

CREATE THE **HIGHEST**, **GRANDEST VISION** POSSIBLE FOR YOUR LIFE. BECAUSE YOU **BECOME** WHAT YOU **BELIEVE**.

Oprah Winfrey
Media Proprietor

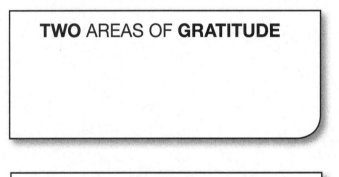

TWO AREAS OF **GRATITUDE**

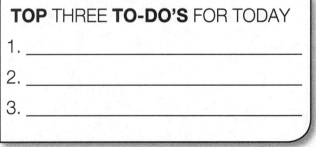

TOP THREE **TO-DO'S** FOR TODAY

1. _____
2. _____
3. _____

A YEAR FROM NOW, YOU WILL **WISH** YOU HAD STARTED **TODAY**.

Karen Lamb
Author

TWO AREAS OF **GRATITUDE**

TOP THREE **TO-DO'S** FOR TODAY

1. _____
2. _____
3. _____

THE BIGGEST **ADVENTURE** YOU CAN TAKE IS TO **LIVE** THE **LIFE** OF YOUR **DREAMS**.

Oprah Winfrey
Media Proprietor

TWO AREAS OF **GRATITUDE**

TOP THREE **TO-DO'S** FOR TODAY

1. _____

2. _____

3. _____

THE THINGS YOU ARE **PASSIONATE** ABOUT ARE NOT **RANDOM**; THEY ARE YOUR **CALLING**.

Fabienne Fredrickson
Professional Business Coach

TWO AREAS OF **GRATITUDE**

TOP THREE **TO-DO'S** FOR TODAY

1. _____
2. _____
3. _____

ONLY I CAN CHANGE MY LIFE. **NO ONE** CAN DO IT FOR ME.

Carol Burnett
Actress, Comedienne, Singer, and Writer

TWO AREAS OF **GRATITUDE**

TOP THREE **TO-DO'S** FOR TODAY

1. _____

2. _____

3. _____

TEN YEARS FROM NOW, **MAKE SURE** YOU CAN SAY THAT **YOU CHOSE YOUR LIFE;** YOU DIDN'T **SETTLE** FOR IT.

Mandy Hale
Author and The Single Woman

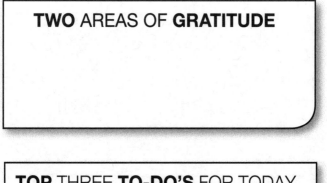

TWO AREAS OF **GRATITUDE**

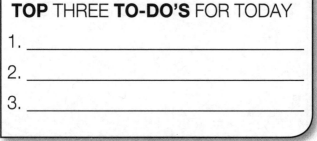

TOP THREE **TO-DO'S** FOR TODAY

1. _____

2. _____

3. _____

LET YOUR **DREAMS** BE **BIGGER** THAN YOUR **FEARS** AND YOUR **ACTIONS** BE **LOUDER** THAN YOUR **WORDS**.

Unknown

TWO AREAS OF **GRATITUDE**

TOP THREE **TO-DO'S** FOR TODAY

1. _____
2. _____
3. _____

ENJOY LIFE NOW.
THIS IS **NOT** A **REHEARSAL**.

Unknown

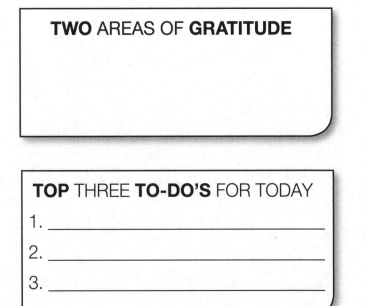

TWO AREAS OF **GRATITUDE**

TOP THREE **TO-DO'S** FOR TODAY

1. _____
2. _____
3. _____

RANDOM **ACT** OF **KINDNESS**

GIVE SOMEONE A
"JUST BECAUSE" GIFT.

CONCLUSION

Take a quick look back through this book. Do you realize that by working through it, you have given your brain 365 doses of inspiration, expressed gratitude for 730 different things, and accomplished 1,095 vital tasks throughout the year? Whoa! Give yourself a big pat on the back for accomplishing so much over the past year.

Isn't it amazing what you can accomplish when you focus your time and attention on the right activities? How positive do you feel? It's pretty tough to dwell on a bad day when you end each day thinking about the things you're most grateful for!

Now, here's a little tip: don't keep this book a secret! Our challenge for you is to think about all the different ways you can allow the imagine–act–inspire concept to positively impact your life. Here are a few ideas:

- **Business owners/professionals:** Share this with your teams to create a more positive, productive environment.

- **Teachers:** Use this book as a tool for your classrooms. You have a great opportunity to impact kids' lives and set them up for success as adults.

- **Parents:** Think about the impact it would have if you did this activity with your entire immediate family. Imagine if every evening at the dinner table, you asked your spouse and kids to list two things they're grateful for. Better yet, get them their own *Imagine. Act. Inspire. Daily Journal* so they can build their best year yet.

Order your new copy of *Imagine. Act. Inspire.* today so we can help you make the next 365 days miraculous. And if you consider yourself a helpful person, give a copy of this book to someone whose life you want to help make even better!

For your continued dose of inspiration, visit our website at daretodreaminspired.com, and join our mailing list.

About Dare to Dream Enterprises and the Authors

Dare to Dream Enterprises provides clarity in a world of chaos so people can focus on the things in life that matter most to them. Dare to Dream supports entrepreneurs in shifting their focus from working *in* their business to working *on* their business, all while helping them realize and build a bigger future so they can take control of their lives.

It is so easy to get caught up in the day-to-day inertia that people often forget to focus on the things that matter most to them in life. That is where Dare to Dream Enterprises comes in. We help you *imagine* the impact you can have on your own life and others, then give you a plan to *act* on it so you can *inspire* those around you to live a life of freedom and abundance.

Brittany Anderson

Cofounder, Dare to Dream Enterprises

Director of Operations and Office Manager, Sweet Financial Services

Brittany is driven by her passion for helping others succeed. There is nothing more motivating to her than seeing a person define what success looks like and then taking the steps to accomplish his or her dream life! This is why she felt the calling to create Dare to Dream Enterprises. Through coaching, she strives to help others move toward the life they can't wait to wake up to.

Brittany began her journey as the COO for Sweet Financial Services, a premiere wealth planning firm in Fairmont, Minnesota, that specializes in helping people live their retirement dreams. In her time at Sweet Financial, she has been a member of The Strategic Coach®, which has helped her uncover her unique ability—engaging teams and motivating people to be the best version of themselves.

Brittany lives in rural Sherburn, Minnesota, with her husband, David, and their daughters, Jersey and Stella. Her definition of success is spending quality time with her family, coaching others to success, working on her latest repurposing project, and spending time outdoors.

Bryan J. Sweet

Cofounder, Dare to Dream Enterprises

Founder and CEO, Sweet Financial Services

Creator of The Dream Architect™

It is because of Bryan's drive to help others fulfill their greatest potential that he has built a successful career helping people realize their biggest dreams. Since the start of his financial services career in 1979, Bryan has specialized in helping individuals accumulate and preserve wealth for retirement and beyond. A native of Fairmont, Minnesota, he earned his master's degree in financial services from The American College in Bryn Mawr, Pennsylvania, before embarking on what would become a lifelong career as a wealth management consultant. He established his own firm, Sweet Financial Services, in 1987 and affiliated with Raymond James in 1989.

Bryan's passion—working with some of his best clients—motivated him to become a member of The Strategic Coach®, which has helped provide the clarity he needed in his business. He found that he works best with high-net-worth business owners who have complex financial needs. In working with this niche, helping move them toward living their retirement dreams, it became evident that all too often, people don't dream big enough—they don't see the forest through the trees. Through Dare to Dream Enterprises, Bryan helps provide clarity in a world of chaos so that people can focus on the things in life that matter most to them.